ENNL HANDBOOK

for

UPPER ADVANCED WRITING

John Sparks and Jean Ady

Portland Community College

KENDALL/HUNT PUBLISHING COMPANY
4050 Westmark Drive　　Dubuque, Iowa 52002

Copyright © 1996, 1999 by John Sparks and Jean Ady

ISBN 0-7872-5778-8

All rights reserved. No part of this publication may be reproduced, stored in a retrieval system, or transmitted, in any form or by any means, electronic, mechanical, photocopying, recording, or otherwise, without the prior written permission of the copyright owner.

Printed in the United States of America
10 9 8 7 6 5 4 3 2 1

TABLE OF CONTENTS

THE UPPER ADVANCED WRITING PAPER

PREPARATION
- Selecting a topic 1
- Outlining 3
- The Thesis Statement 5
- The Introduction 9
- The Body Paragraphs 11
- Topic Sentences 13
- The Conclusion 15
- The Title 17
- Formating Your Paper 19
- Writing Drafts 21
- Review of steps in preparing a paper 21

RHETORICAL STYLES 22
- Description Essay 22
- Cause/Effect Essay 30
- Discussion Essay 36
- Classification Essay 43
- Problem/Solution Essay 49
- Extended Definition Essay 55
- Argument Essay 61

IN-CLASS WRITING 71
- Purpose of In-class Writing 71
- Preparation 71
- Reading Response 72

THE RESEARCH PAPER
- Purpose of the Research Paper 75
- Plagiarism 76
- The Learning Resource Center (LRC) 77
- Note-taking 78
- Quoting 82
- Paraphrasing 84
- Summarizing 88
- Documentation 93
- Special punctuation notes 94
- Illustrations 95
- The List of Works Cited 97
- Research Paper Proposal 101
- Review of steps in preparing the research paper 102
- Example of a student research paper 103

PREFACE

This handbook is designed for ENNL students in Upper Advanced Writing. The <u>ENNL Handbook for Upper Advanced Writing</u> grew out of <u>The ENNL Handbook for the Research Paper</u> and the materials prepared by ENNL instructors for writing assignments at the Upper Advanced level.

We would like to thank Roxanne Hill, Claudia Nawas, Christina Sparks and Kate Gawf for their valuable suggestions during the creation of this handbook, and Janice Ruhl, who did much of the typing for the original edition. We are of course grateful to those students from our classes, as well as those who had work published in the <u>ENNL Ambassador</u>, whose assignments are used as examples.

In addition, we would like to thank the following for giving permission to reprint materials in the Handbook: Gruner + Jahr USA Publishing (<u>Parents</u> magazine) and Albert Shanker: <u>On Campus</u>.

John Sparks and Jean Ady
ENNL Instructors
Sylvania Campus, P.C.C.

Second edition,
December 1998

To the Instructor: Suggestions for Using the Handbook

The nature of the ENNL curriculum necessitates the use of a handbook such as this one, together with a grammar textbook, if the entire ENL 262 curriculum is to be addressed.

Although this handbook conforms to the ENNL curriculum, it is not exhaustive and, indeed, has been kept to a certain length to reduce the costs for students. Instructors should provide supplementary materials as needed, including other student essay examples from their own classes and supplementary exercises on the writing process.

In this edition, we are not providing blank outlines for each essay. There are various approaches to outlining and we feel that instructors should introduce a variety of prewriting tasks. In addition, an outline form often leads to very structured essays containing the exact number of paragraphs in the outline, no more and no fewer!

The research paper section of the handbook seems lengthy considering the fact that we only write one research paper at this level. It is not intended that the students memorize documentation conventions: the handbook is designed to serve as a reference. Indeed, it should prove useful to students in the years after they leave ENNL. Students should be cautioned, however, that different disciplines and different instructors advocate conventions other than the M.L.A. style we follow here.

THE UPPER ADVANCED WRITING PAPER

PREPARATION

Selecting a Topic

When selecting a topic for a paper, it is important to **narrow** the subject. A large, very general subject, for example "My city," cannot be dealt with in very much detail in a short paper of two to four typed pages. Therefore, it is necessary to narrow your topic so that you can supply as many interesting details as possible and treat the subject **in depth**.

Example: Let's take the topic "My City" and see how it can be narrowed.

Step 1: general subject	My City: Portland
Step 2: more specific subject	Portland: the downtown area
Step 3: even more specific subject	Pioneer Square
Step 4:	Pioneer Square at midday
Step 5:	Pioneer Square at midday during the summer
Step 6:	Pioneer Square at midday during the summer looking out from Starbuck's coffee shop

By going through a step-by-step approach to narrowing the topic, you can find a suitable subject for a short paper. Notice that the final topic (Step 6) gives you a very specific focus for a description essay in terms of place: "Pioneer Square"; time: "midday"; season: "summer"; and perspective: "from Starbuck's coffee shop."

In addition, while selecting a topic, you need to be acutely aware of your **audience**. For the purpose of your ENNL writing, the audience consists of your peers (classmates) and your instructor. Therefore, you need to select a topic which will be interesting for your teacher and your classmates.

Exercise 1

Try to narrow the following topic in six steps.

Step 1:   Economic problems

Step 2:

Step 3:

Step 4:

Step 5:

Step 6:

Exercise 2

Now try to narrow this topic:

Step 1:   A wedding ceremony

Step 2:

Step 3:

Step 4:

Step 5:

Step 6:

Outlining

When you have done all your thinking and perhaps some reading for the paper, it is time to make a brief outline. This outline should reflect all the topical divisions of the paper, as well as the paper's organization.

Below is a sample paper outline.

Topic: "Should there be a sales tax in Oregon?"

1. What is a sales tax?
    A. definition
    B. states which have sales tax

2. Arguments for a sales tax
    A. increases revenue to compensate for Measure 5
    B. spreads tax burden equally according to personal expenditure
    C. taxes all people shopping in Oregon, including foreigners and visitors from out-of-state

3. Arguments against a sales tax
    A. merchants say a sales tax will discourage consumers
    B. additional tax is not needed: budget-cutting is needed

4. Refutation of arguments against sales tax

5. Conclusion: Oregon should institute a sales tax

We can see from the outline that this essay will probably consist of nine paragraphs: 1A, 1B, 2A, 2B, 2C, 3A, 3B, 4, 5.

Sample essay outline

Title: _____

First paragraph (Introduction): Think of an interesting anecdote, quote, example, etc., to begin. Write the **thesis statement**.

_____

_____

First body paragraph: Topic sentence + details and examples

_____

_____

_____

Next paragraph: Topic sentence + details and examples

_____

_____

_____

Next paragraph: Topic sentence + details and examples

_____

_____

_____

Final paragraph: (Conclusion): Give a summarizing statement, opinion, prediction, or solution.

_____

PLEASE NOTE: A good essay at this level could have as few as four paragraphs or as many as seven, eight, nine, or more! Do not try to fit all your ideas into a five-paragraph outline.

The Thesis Statement

Now that you have a good idea of what you are going to write about, you need to write a **thesis statement**. The thesis statement is usually the final sentence in the introductory paragraph. It declares the author's purpose in writing the paper.

A thesis statement can be defined as <u>an opinion which can be defended</u>. It should tell the reader the <u>main idea</u> of the paper. It is <u>not</u> a question, but a clear statement of opinion which can be supported by the body of your essay. It should:

1. consist of a single grammatical sentence;
2. mention your specific topic;
3. (optional) contain the aspects of your topic (e.g. the different causes of a situation);
4. reveal your <u>purpose</u>;
5. be the <u>final sentence</u> of your introductory paragraph.

Remember that you should select a thesis (topic and purpose) which will be <u>interesting</u>, <u>informative</u>, and <u>thought-provoking</u> for your teacher and your classmates. You will be supporting your thesis in later paragraphs with facts, statistics, anecdotes, examples, and other relevant details.

<u>What is **NOT** a good thesis statement</u>

At this level of writing, please refrain from choosing a topic which is already very well-known to your audience, or which may be too obvious, or uninteresting, for example:

"There are several steps involved in changing the oil in your car."

"Drinking alcohol may cause traffic accidents, family problems, and health problems."

"Los Angeles and Portland are very different cities"

In addition, avoid <u>vague</u> or general thesis statements, for example:

NOT: "Dai Hoc Tong Hop in Saigon and P.C.C. Sylvania in Portland have many similarities and differences."

BUT: "Dai Hoc Tong Hop and P.C.C. Sylvania are considered fine colleges in their respective countries, but they differ considerably in terms of their course offerings, entrance requirements, available equipment, and campus design."

At this level of writing, a thesis statement should **NOT** represent one of the following:

a) a well-known fact

"Portland has four seasons: winter, spring, summer, and fall." (Everyone in your audience knows this.)

b) a belief

"Homosexuality will destroy society." (You cannot prove this point in an essay or convince others who don't have the same beliefs as you do).

c) a question

"Should teachers give students grades?" (Your thesis should be a statement of your opinion on a subject).

d) a personal expression of intent (in expository essays)

"Now I am going to tell you about the problem of smoking." (In expository writing, you need to leave out the word 'I' and be more objective).

e) a blanket statement

"Children in America watch too much T.V." (Use modals such as 'may' or 'might' and qualifying adjectives such as 'many' or 'some').

Examples of thesis statements

Descriptive process: *
"A wedding in the Georgian Republic is a spectacular ceremony which is prepared in several elaborate steps."

Descriptive narrative: *
"When I was a child, I especially enjoyed the times that my uncle Woo took me fishing on the South China Sea."

Cause:
"Calcutta is an overcrowded city because of increasing immigration from the rural areas of West Bengal."

Effect:
"Requiring ENNL students to take Reading, Speaking, and Writing classes will ensure that students are well-prepared in all the communication skills which are critical to success in college."

Classification:
"Book lovers can be categorized into three major groups: those who buy books to decorate their homes; those who read their books once and then forget them; and those who treat their books like revered companions."

Problem/solution:
"The theft of stereos from cars is a serious problem in the Portland area; however, there are several ways in which we can control the situation."

Discussion:
"There is serious disagreement about the morality of Oregon's Assisted Suicide Law."

Definition:
"The 1954 Supreme Court decision to declare racially segregated schools unconstitutional was the logical base for the civil rights movement."

Argument:
"The U.S. should consider instituting a same-sex public school system because this would allow students to study without being distracted by the opposite sex."

---

* Descriptive and narrative essays do not require an obvious thesis statement.
However, the <u>thesis</u> (topic and controlling idea) should be clear to the reader.

Exercise 3

Try to think of a suitable thesis statement for the following topics.

1. Eating at fast-food restaurants

2. Different kinds of computer users

3. The pros and cons of issuing condoms to high school students

4. Walking dogs without a leash

5. Your favorite place at the Oregon Coast

6. The funniest event of your childhood

7. Grading practices at P.C.C.

8. A New Year's celebration

9. Sending a manned mission to Mars

10. The effects of working part-time and taking a full load of classes

The Introduction

An introductory paragraph in an essay usually comes in two parts: first, the attention-getting ideas which introduce the topic; these are followed by the **thesis statement**.

Writing a good introduction to an essay takes skill and careful thought. It is important to write a paragraph that will convince the reader that the essay is worth reading. YOUR TITLE IS **NOT** YOUR INTRODUCTION. Some effective ways to introduce an essay are to:

1. use an appropriate quotation;
2. write about an interesting incident related to the topic;
3. use an anecdote (yours or someone else's);
4. identify yourself as an expert on the topic;
5. use facts and statistics about the topic.

The introduction should not seem 'tacked-on': it must be an integral part of your essay. The length of your introduction must not seem out of proportion with the rest of your essay.

Poor introductions (first sentences of an essay)

1. The very general, very shallow statement:

   "Food is a very important thing in human life."

2. The made-up conversation:

   "Recently, I was chatting with my high school friends about how to classify teachers in terms of their classroom methodology."

3. A leap right into the topic:

   "At P.C.C., eating and drinking should be permitted during class."

   (This would be all right for a thesis statement, but is not a good first sentence)

4. The personal question:

   "What do you think about a sales tax in Oregon?"

5. The personal opinion:

   "I think that people should not have more than one child."

Here are some examples of introductory paragraphs to student papers; the <u>thesis statement</u> is underlined.

Topic: "The Homeless in Japan"

I remember a homeless man whom I saw almost every morning on the way to school in my hometown of Fukuoka, in southern Japan. Crossing through a narrow park in a valley surrounded by high-rise apartments, I would see a man who wore a dusty, old-fashioned business jacket and a very large pair of pants full of holes. He had long, gray hair and a beard, and his gloomy eyes were like those of a dead fish. In the park, he read books almost every day, sitting up straight on a bench. He was one of the educated 'furuosha', or homeless people, whose number is estimated to be 100,000 in Japan. <u>The furuosha have become homeless because of their inability to cope with modern, fast-paced society.</u>

Yukiko Higuma

Topic: "The Causes of Overcrowding in Bangkok"

Thailand is an independent, developing nation in Asia. Thailand's richest natural resource lies in its agricultural potential. However, some parts of the country, especially the northeast and the north, are still poor. Many people have moved from these areas to the capital, Bangkok. As a result, Bangkok has become seriously overpopulated. <u>There are three major reasons for the problem of overcrowding in Bangkok: large numbers of rural people have moved to the city to seek opportunities; laborers are in great demand due to the rapidly industrializing economy; and natural disasters in the countryside often force people to relocate.</u>

Chintana Apinantpreeda

Topic: "Espresso Drinkers"

Anywhere you go in the city, there are Espresso signs. Espresso is really popular. Are people drinking Espresso because it is a trendy thing to do, or do they really like its taste? Why do people pay so much money for a little drink? A couple of years ago, I purchased an Espresso machine for my delicatessen. I then had fun observing the customers who came to drink Espresso. <u>I soon noticed that there are three different kinds of people who drink Espresso.</u>

Sung Phillips

The Body Paragraphs

The body paragraphs are the longest section of your essay. They should make up at least 75 percent of the total length of your paper. Each paragraph should contain one **main idea** and should be developed with such details as statistics, facts, anecdotes, examples, stories of personal experience, descriptive details and explanations.

Each body paragraph usually contains a **topic sentence**, which is often the first sentence in the paragraph. Topic sentences sometimes begin with a transition word or phrase, such as 'On the other hand', 'As a result', 'First', 'Second', 'Finally'.

Body paragraphs move from **general** to **specific** information. After the topic sentence, there may be a brief explanation, but then the paragraph should be developed using interesting details. A body paragraph should be several sentences in length. One or two sentences does not make a paragraph. Remember that all the information in each of the body paragraphs must relate directly to your **thesis**.

Here are some examples of body paragraphs; the topic sentence is underlined.

Topic: "Should Our Mother Go Back to Vietnam?"

My brothers had the following reasons for their position. First, my mother's life in America is boring. She doesn't go to work because she doesn't speak English. She stays at home and takes care of her grandchildren, who bother her all day. When my mother was in Vietnam, she visited her friends and relatives often. She has no friends or relatives in Oregon. She really feels sad and lonely. Second, if my mother lived in Vietnam, she could go wherever she wanted by herself. In America, she can't communicate with other people outside the family and she can't drive. Every time she wants to go out, she has to ask us. Sometimes she doesn't dare ask us because she knows that we are busy or tired. Once, one of my brothers had promised to take my mother to a Vietnamese market on a Saturday. However, the night before, he got to bed late. On Saturday, my mother saw him sleeping so well that she didn't wake him up, so she didn't go to the market. Third, while the weather in Oregon is cold, the weather in Vietnam is warm and very healthy for old people. When my mother lived in Vietnam, she was seldom sick. Since she has lived in America, she has often been sick.

Thanh Thuy Tran

Topic: "Stereotypes of Hispanics in the U.S."

<u>Another factor that has contributed to the devaluation of the image of the Hispanic relates to personality.</u> The nature of the Latin American is different from that of the North American. It is more social. This characteristic can be seen as positive in that people are more relaxed and tend to feel closer to one another, united. Unfortunately, when a crowd of people who feel oppressed by the system gets together, the results may not be very positive. The formation of gangs and riots, for instance, and the efforts to make easy money even if it means being an outlaw are the most notorious effects.

Jose Higa

Topic: "Great Feelings from Great Paintings"

<u>American folk-art paintings, such as some painted by Charles Wysocki or Mattie Lou O'Kelley, always make me feel happy when I look at them</u>. There are always houses, trees, flowers, farms, happy folks - many beautiful things in the pictures. I learn about the changes in the land and the different seasons. Everyone is living together in harmony. Men are working on the farm or making handicrafts. Women are sitting together, making many different kinds of fruit pies in the kitchen: apple pies, cherry pies, pumpkin pies, berry pies - they look delicious! On holidays, everyone gathers around in a very big house and has a party. Some people are dancing or looking after their babies. Children are playing and running around the house. Some also try to steal food from the kitchen when everyone is busy. When I look at these paintings, I can feel their happiness. It is just like listening to some soft music. I wish I were living in their world.

Kwong Ngai Hung

Topic: "Marijuana as Medicine"

<u>One of marijuana's therapeutic benefits is its ability to suppress the nausea and vomiting suffered by many patients undergoing anti-cancer chemotherapy.</u> Conventional antiemetic medications often fail to control these symptoms, and the main active substance in marijuana, delta-9tetrahydrocannibol (THC) taken orally appeared to be less effective than crude marijuana. Marijuana's vapour is easily absorbed and acts quickly. Moreover, other cannabinoids in the marijuana plant may modify the action of THC (Grinspoon 1876). Users can fine-tune the dose for themselves. Having marijuana cigarettes under their control allows chemotherapy patients to ease their feelings of helplessness ("Marijuana as a Medicine"). In a 1990 poll, more than 40% of American oncologists revealed that they had suggested that patients smoke marijuana for the relief of nausea induced by chemotherapy ("Cannabis and Medicine").

Margarita Vainiene

Topic Sentences

Use topic sentences for the body paragraphs of your essays. Topic sentences are more general sentences which tell the reader the main idea of the paragraph. A topic sentence is often the first sentence in the paragraph. Sometimes, it might be the second sentence if the first sentence is transitional. A topic sentence may also appear later in the paragraph.

Exercise 4

Write appropriate topic sentences for the following paragraphs taken from student essays:

1. _____

   _____ . You feel like an animal before the hunt. You are excited as if you were experiencing a soccer game inside your stomach. The wrestling mat rests on the middle of the gym floor, and the whole room looks like an ancient Roman gladiator arena. An eager crowd sits around it, waiting for the circus to begin. You sniff the atmosphere around you and you smell blood.

   Dmitrij Jemeljanov

2. _____

   _____ . They said that they would not allow their children to watch violent cartoons. When asked about those programs, one of them said: "As the mother of three boys, I have seen how these programs affect not only how they play with other children, but how they view the world. These shows teach children how to solve problems with violence." Another parent complained: "My child has watched cartoon shows such as G.I. Joe and The Master of the Universe, and his behavior is markedly more aggressive and violent after viewing these shows."

   Buoi Vo

3. _____

   _____ . For most people, the lack of privacy presents the most problems because people cannot do things which they might do if they lived alone. For example, inviting friends to stay overnight, or having a party until the morning light is not possible if one's roommate has a problem with sleeping. Even insignificant matters, like leaving a dirty dish in the sink or forgetting to put the garbage out in the morning could lead to an argument. If one roommate is unable to pay the rent and utilities, the other could get into trouble with the landlord as well.

   Dora Papay

4. _____

_____ . These mothers are worried about everything. They ask so many questions, like, "Is the baby alive?"; "Is it a boy or a girl?"; "Is the baby healthy?"; Is it a human or an alien?"; "What will my husband say if the baby is ugly?" These are the negative thoughts of some mothers-to-be, especially when their due dates are getting closer.

Sima Vossough

Exercise 5

On a separate sheet of paper, write short paragraphs, with appropriate details and examples, to support the following topic sentences.

1. Some immigrants are apathetic about learning English.

2. On the positive side, we can cross borders through the Internet.

3. Suddenly, we heard a slight noise from the bushes ahead of us.

4. There are several simple steps that I follow in order to make my English as understandable as possible to native speakers.

5. Since many people have lost their jobs because of the economic crisis in Mexico, crime and violence have increased enromously.

6. Requiring uniforms in public schools would ensure that students from wealthy families would not look any different from students from poor families.

7. Some people simply enjoy meaningless and endless conversations on the phone.

8. Parents should ask themselves the question: "Are we doing damage to our children by putting them into day care during the first year of their lives?"

The Conclusion

The concluding paragraph of your essay is an integral part of the paper, just like the introduction. Your conclusion should be brief and should also relate directly to your **thesis**. A conclusion should **NOT** introduce a new aspect of the topic or a new example. A good conclusion may involve:

1. a restatement of your thesis or opinion (in different words);
2. a prediction (what may happen in the future);
3. a summary of your position or argument;
4. a suggestion, piece of advice, or proposed solution (briefly) to the problem discussed in your paper.

Here are some examples of concluding paragraphs:

Topic: "Government Workers in China"

    These three kinds of persons exist in every government unit. The flatterers are a minority because they are dishonest, and most people hate being such persons. The numbers of hard workers are few because many people reluctantly restrain themselves from spending their precious time or energy just on the hope of promotion. People in the middle are the majority because many people want to live for themselves. To be specific, as either way of getting a promotion, flattering or hard-working, is against their will or hurts their self respect, many people would rather live at ease or be poor than make any effort to get a promotion. This choice, at least, makes them feel they are human beings; they are the masters of their own lives rather than slaves of somebody else.

                                                                                          Yanni Yang

Topic: "The Philippine-American War"

    Americans seem to think that they know best for everyone else, and American history teaches Americans to believe this. We Filipinos have the idea of a personal debt of honor, so this keeps us from recognizing the truth. We feel that we owe America everything that we are, so we are not interested in discovering the truth about American friendship. For example, I was raised to think of Admiral Dewey as a Philippine hero. Now, I'm angry and sad to learn that Admiral Dewey was a traitor to Filipinos by lying to General Aguinaldo and turning against Filipinos. I was shocked to learn that over 216,000 Filipinos were killed during the war, but only 4,200 American soldiers died. This is something I did not think America would do.

                                                                     Mary Jane Harvey

Topic: "The Celebration of Têt"

Têt remains the most important festival for the Vietnamese who think that this is the time to pay special respect and gratitude to the elders, masters, and benefactors. Têt is the time to take a pause from work and enjoy fully some good moments with family, relatives, and friends. Têt is also the time of mixing the blooming of flowers and harmonizing of nature with the feeling of anxieties and hopes, joy and happiness of all Vietnamese people. In America, everything connected with the Têt has changed, but we try to do our best to welcome Têt.

Quy Cao

Topic: "The Reasons for Overcrowding in Seoul"

Overpopulation is a problem that everyone in the world has to think about. If we just do nothing to prevent the world from being overpopulated, the world as we know it will be destroyed. The solution in Korea is to evenly develop the country, not just the capital city. In addition, the government needs to give benefits to farmers and small towns. This would help to solve the overpopulation problem in Seoul.

Hui Chin Yi

Topic: "One Extraordinary Chinese Meal"

After this unforgettable dinner, I really appreciated Auntie Lee. Because of that dinner, Chuck began to understand more about Chinese food, Chinese tradition, and his Chinese girlfriend. He is no longer afraid to read those chicken palms anymore. Besides that, when I decided to have some real Chinese food for dinner, he said simply, "I will try it as long as it is clean."

Fung Lam Chung

The Title

It is harder than you think to make a good title for your essay. A title should be **short**: it is **not a full sentence** and may omit some some function words, such as articles, helping verbs, verb 'to be', or pronouns. Good titles do not necessarily define your exact topic. Rather, they will use an **intriguing** or **'catchy'** phrase to make the reader want to read the essay. Titles often pose a question that the reader will want to see answered in the essay.

Examples of 'catchy' titles

a. for an essay about students who study hard in high school:

 "Why Don't We Just 'Goof Off'?"

b. for an essay about the kinds of people who eat popcorn at movie theaters:

 "Salt and Butter, Please"

Sometimes titles can come in two parts, a 'catchy' phrase followed by a **colon** and a topic statement, for example:

c. for an essay about the reasons for poor eating habits:

 "Junk Diets: Why We Eat Trash"

d. for an essay about the problem of dogs that bark all night:

 "Muzzle Your Mutt: Taking Care of a Neighborhood Nuisance."

Try to make your title interesting. It should catch the reader's eye and make them want to read further.

Examples of poor titles

i. Don't make the kind of essay you are writing into a title, e.g.:

 "Discussion Essay"

ii. Don't make the title of your essay too obvious, e.g.:

 "Parking Permits at P.C.C."

iii. Don't make your title into a complete sentence, e.g.

 "Doctor-assisted Suicide Should Be Against the Law"

Remember that your title should be **centered on the page** and should be in the same **plain, 12-point font** as the rest of your essay. All words in the title should be capitalized except for articles, conjunctions, and prepositions of two and three letters.

Exercise 6

Think of some good titles for the following topics:

1. A descriptive essay about Multnomah Falls.

2. An essay about the causes of roommate arguments.

3. An essay about the effects of working full-time and taking care of young children.

4. An essay about the advantages and disadvantages of making your children speak your native language at home.

5. An essay about the different kinds of people who go to the zoo.

6. An essay about finding a parking space at P.C.C. - Sylvania.

7. An essay about the Apollo 11 moon landing.

8. An essay which advocates shortening the regular work week from 40 to 30 hours.

9. An essay which supports charging a toll on Interstate 5 through Portland.

10. An essay which is against state-controlled alcohol sales.

Formating your paper

Fonts

If you are typing your paper on a computer, select a font which is easily legible and of appropriate size (12 point). The Geneva or New York fonts are modern, not too small, and easy to read, for example:

Geneva 12-point:

He thought he saw an Elephant,
   That practised on a fife:

New York 12-point:

He looked again, and found it was
   A letter from his wife.

Please use the same font at 12-point size for your <u>whole paper</u>, including the title. Do not use bold lettering, italics, or shadow lettering, such as the following, in your paper.

Don't type this: *Gee, isn't this cool?*

or this: **Wow, this is really smashing!!!!!!!**

Margins

Leave a one inch margin on **all sides** of your paper. Set your margins on the computer before you begin typing.

Spacing

Always use double-spacing when typing a paper. Select the double-space option from the menu bar on your computer before you begin typing the paper. Everything on the title page should also be double-spaced.

Type only on **one side** of the page.

Title Page

The first page of your paper should include the following information: your name, course number, the name of your instructor, and date (all in the top left corner); the title of your paper (centered); the introductory paragraph, with thesis statement; and the beginning of your text.

Here is an example of the top part of a title page:

Van Tran

ENL 262

Instructor: John Sparks

November 15th, 1994

The Plight of the Hong Kong Boat People

On Monday, Feb. 25, 1994, a 31-nation meeting held in Geneva decided that boat people from communist nations like Vietnam no longer would get special treatment, and they could be shipped home by host countries if they couldn't prove that they would suffer persecution in Vietnam: "Only 8000 of the 60,000 Vietnamese refugees still living in camps in Hong Kong, Malaysia, Indonesia, the Philippines, and Japan have valid fears of persecution and can be expected to be resettled. The rest will have to go back to Vietnam" (Higgins 67).

I'm also a Vietnamese refugee, and I'm luckier than those left in refugee camps

---

Pagination

Starting from the **second page** of the paper, number all pages in the upper right-hand corner, 1/2 inch from the top and 1 inch from the right margin. **Do not number the title page.** Use the header function on your word-processing software to insert your page numbers.

Type your last name before the page number, in case your pages are lost, for example:

Nakazaki 5

Writing Drafts

It probably takes at least three drafts to write a good paper.

1. The "rough" draft

Start writing your paper with the outline and the notes in front of you. Don't worry too much about your language in this draft. Just try to get all your ideas down on paper in an organized form. Once you have completed the "rough" draft, you can go back and correct errors. Right now, the most important point to remember is to check your **organization**.

2. The second draft

Rewrite the paper and type it, using a computer or a typewriter, making sure that organization and most language problems are corrected. Please type double-spaced and follow the proper form for a typed paper (see "Title page", p. 111). If you are writing a research paper, be sure that you have the **correct references** for any quoting or paraphrasing you may have done. This will probably be the first draft that you hand in to your instructor.

3. The final draft

Review your instructor's corrections and comments. Correct **any additional errors** and make your final adjustments. Retype the paper.

Review of steps in preparing a paper

- I.   **Brainstorm and select a topic.**
- II.   **Narrow the topic.**
- III.   **Write an outline.**
- IV.   **Prepare the thesis statement.**
- V.   **Write the "rough" draft, with introduction, body paragraphs, and conclusion.**
- VI.   **Correct the "rough" draft and type a second draft to hand in to your instructor.**
- VII.   **Revise and type the final draft, paying close attention to your instructor's comments.**

RHETORICAL STYLES

Description essay

A description essay can be <u>objective</u> or <u>subjective</u>. An objective description describes what anybody can experience. It contains facts, not value judgments or emotions. A subjective description is an individual impression: It conveys the feelings and opinions of the writer.

Follow these points when writing a description:

1. Your introductory paragraph should set the time, place, personalities, and <u>main idea</u> of your description.

2. When you describe a person, place, or object, you want the reader to be able to <u>experience</u> your topic through your writing.

3. Select a topic which is narrow: for example, instead of writing about a city, describe the Saturday market in the city, or better still, one or two stalls at the market; instead of describing an entire house, write only about the balcony or the back yard.

4. A good description has many specific details. The details should be arranged in some kind of order and the description should be cohesive: that is, all the details should relate to each other in some way. Your perceptions, or point of view, should be clear. Dynamics, or movement, in your description should not be confusing.

5. Don't try to describe everything about your topic. Be <u>selective</u>: choose only those aspects which are interesting and which are related to your <u>main idea</u>.

6. In a good description, the writer should attempt to appeal to the five senses: sight, smell, touch, hearing, and taste. Try to evoke colors, odors, emotions. How does light, or time of day, affect the mood or atmosphere? What does a color, odor, sound, or a certain light suggest or symbolize to you?

7. Use metaphors and similes, for example:
   "It made a noise like the squeaking of a newborn mouse." (simile)
   "The sea tossed in its dark sheets, restless before the dawn." (metaphor)
   "Her skin was hard and wrinkled like a dried fig that had been stored for difficult times." (simile)
   "The evening cooled the land and the wind fell asleep in the oaks." (metaphor)

8. Use a variety of adjectives and action verbs.

9. Use past tenses when describing a scene from your past. Use present tenses when describing a place that you continue to visit or use. Always use the past when describing events which have been completed.

10. Your essay should have a controlling idea or message which may be best presented in the conclusion. Why did you choose this topic? What special meaning does it have for you? Your main idea should be briefly mentioned in the introduction. (topic sentence).

Topics for descriptive writing

Descriptive narration essay

A descriptive narration will tell a story, usually from the past, but will be illustrated by many descriptive details and anecdotes. Possible topics might include:

A childhood activity, such as having a snowball fight
An interesting experience described as a sequence of events
The story of an interesting trip
A favorite natural place
A place from your childhood, such as your grandmother's house
An interesting place, such as a crowded bar or disco
An interesting building, bridge, room, etc.

Descriptive process essay

A descriptive process essay will outline a series of steps or events. For each step, the writer gives details and examples which help to illustrate the scene. The following topics would be appropriate:

An aspect of a traditional ceremony from your culture
A religious ritual
A modern ceremony, such as graduation
A series of events leading to a memorable conclusion
A descriptive explanation of how to operate a machine
How to perform a complicated task, e.g. prepare for a party, write a novel, rehearse for a
    role in a play, judge a fashion show, prepare for a mountain-climbing expedition,
    hunt a wild animal, do some kind of farm work.

Description: Using Specific Words

In order to make your writing more interesting, try to use very specific words.

Vague, general sentence: We saw some nice things in the shop.

Specific and focused: The window display in Hughie's Bookstore emphasized cookbooks with recipes from exotic lands in Asia and the Middle East.

Exercise 7

Rewrite the following sentences using interesting vocabulary and more specific words. Add adjectives and adverbs where you can.

1. After swimming, we ate some good food.

2. At sunrise, we heard the birds sing.

3. He was driving a nice-looking car.

4. The old person walked slowly down the road.

5. The moon appeared over the tops of the trees.

6. The truck moved down the road.

7. A person was in front of the building.

8. We had an exciting time at the party.

9. It was a nice day.

10. She was wearing a beautiful dress.

ENL 262: UPPER ADVANCED WRITING Name: _____

Peer Review: Description Essay

Writer: _____

Title: _____

1. What is the topic of the essay?

2. Is the focus of the essay narrow enough, or do you think the author should narrow the topic more? Do you have any suggestions?

3. Does the writer get your attention introduction? Why/Why not?

4. Write down two or three similes or metaphors that the writer uses.

5. What is the best part of the essay? Why?

6. What is the least effective aspect of this essay? How do you suggest that the writer change it?

7. On the back of this sheet, write a paragraph which details your response to this essay.

Descriptive narration

An Unforgettable Trip

    While waiting to pick up a close friend recently at Portland's Union Station, I was reminded of an unforgettable train trip that my mother and I took in 1981 to visit my father, who was living in a re-education camp in northern Vietnam. Our trip from Binh Trieu Station to my father's camp taught me the strength of my mother's love for my father through hard, strange, and stressful times.

    On December 20, my mother and I carefully packed rice, sugar, salt, milk, meat, and several kinds of dried fish to take to my father, who was being held in Hanoi. Early that morning, we rushed off to Binh Trieu, a small train station near my house in southern Vietnam. After buying two tickets, we got on the train, found two seats, and stored our luggage. It took us almost four days to get to Hanoi, arriving in the evening.

    When we got to this city, which we had never visited before, we felt like fish out of water. After getting off the train, most of the other passengers quickly dispersed because they knew exactly where they wanted to go. We, on the other hand, felt lost because we didn't know how to get to my father's camp or what transportation we should take. Then a man standing beside a motorcycle with a small trailer attached came up and asked my mother, "Where are you going?" When my mother explained that we were going to visit my father at Hanoi's re-education camp, he smiled and said, "Don't worry. I'll take both of you. It takes about two hours." He helped us put our luggage into the trailer. Finally, we arrived at my father's camp at midnight, and my mother paid the driver.

    We were taken to a cottage that had no furniture or electricity. There were some candles burning on the walls. The air in this low-roofed cottage was very humid. Over thirty people were waiting there to visit husbands, sons, or other relatives. Because of the long trip, we were quite tired, so we fell asleep on the ground almost immediately. The next morning, the director of the camp came and told my mother that we had to wait at least three days to see my father, that we could see him for only one hour, and that it was an annoyance for him to have to arrange for visits on such short notice.

    My mother and I were deeply disappointed, but we waited and slept in the cottage without blankets. The evenings were cool and the nights rather cold. As a result, I got sick, and my mother had to stay up at night to take care of me. My mother expected me to improve, but I only got worse, so she cried and requested that the director allow us to visit my father sooner than scheduled. Finally, he reluctantly agreed.

    I had tried to imagine my father's appearance and voice, but it was hard because I hadn't seen him for eight years. Although I was sick, I sat up in a chair in a small room beside the cottage waiting with my mother to see my father. At the same time, seven other women and four other children were sitting around waiting for their relatives. Everyone was silent; we just looked at each other without talking.

Suddenly, the door opened. Eight men stepped in and sat down face to face with their wives, children, and friends. At that important moment, my father, who was thin with darkened skin, sat opposite us. My parents looked at each other but didn't talk for a while. When I looked around, I saw other people looking at each other without speaking. My parents had tears in their eyes. My father held and kissed my mother's hand. A little later, my father held me tightly, kissed me on the forehead, and asked me many everyday questions such as, "How are you? Have you been good? How is school? What are you doing in your leisure time? Did you go somewhere last summer?" He listened to every single answer, touched my face, and reminded me of something he always included in his letters: "You must obey your mother and help her in any way you can and not forget to write to me whenever you have time."

    I was deeply moved by my father's appearance, voice, and words. The visiting hour went by so fast that I couldn't believe it. However, I felt very satisfied and happy to have seen my father. After that, my mother kept visiting my father twice a year until he was released on June 8, 1987. My family came to the United States in 1993. Since then, my father has been working for an electric company, and my mother has been staying home taking care of my father, brother, older sister, and me. I'm often reminded of our amazing trip and the strength of my parents' love. I thank God for giving me wonderful parents who never stopped believing in their future.

                                                                    Kim Dang

Descriptive Process

Quinceañera

    "Quince Años," which means fifteen years in Spanish, has been the most significant and popular celebration for girls in Mexico for years. It is a coming of age commemoration in which girls pass from childhood to adulthood. "Quince Años" is the dream of all girls, so at an early age (eight or nine years old) they become anxious to be the "Quince Añera." A lot of time and money are spent for this celebration, but it is repaid in the form of the emotions and satisfaction the girl feels when her dreams become reality. She is the center of attention for her special day; she dresses like a queen, and she receives plenty of presents.

    The activities on the day of the celebration start early. The "Quinceañera" goes to a beauty salon where she gets her hair fixed and gets made-up. She is dressed in a beautiful dress designed with lace, satin, and velvet. Usually the color is white, pink, or sky blue. Meanwhile, the mother fixes the food, the father cleans the house, and the brothers decorate it with coils made of bright-colored paper.

    By noon, the "Quinceañera," parents, and relatives go to church. The priest gives a sermon to the "Quinceañera" and blesses her. A big reception, which sometimes has a hundred or more people, is waiting for them when they return from church. The main food that is served is "Mole," which is a spicy sauce made with eight different kinds of peppers. After dinner, everybody dances and drinks. The most important part comes in the middle of the night when a show previously practiced is performed by the "Quinceañera" and her chambelanes. The "Chambelanes," have practiced their unique waltz for three or four weeks. The chambelanes wear suits, gloves, and hats; they carry canes.

    The "Quinceañera" also dances with her father and close relatives. The father gives a speech in which he mentions how proud he is of her, how much he loves her, and how she can be a good woman. Some fathers put such feeling and emphasis into their speech that the "Quinceañera" and guests are deeply touched. Finally, everybody toasts the "Quinceañera" at the culmination of the celebration.

    Even though such a ceremony costs a lot of money and time, parents do not resent the expense, probably because they know how important it is for a girl to be "Quinceañera." They make any sacrifice in order to make their daughter's dream a reality.

Esteban Ortiz

Cause /Effect essay

A cause/effect essay is an explanation of why something happened or why something is happening and/or the results of this event. Some essays focus on causes, others on effects; many discuss both. At this level, you should focus on either causes <u>or</u> effects, but not both.

It is important to give careful thought to the planning stage of this essay. Before beginning the composition, list the various causes or effects that occur to you, consider the probability of each one, and decide on the most likely explanation or explanations. When you are not positive that your explanation is accurate, you should use terms like "maybe", "possibly", or "probably".

Your essay should be structured as follows:

Introduction:	Anecdote or definition of topic; brief summary of causes if you are writing an effect essay, or effects if you are writing a cause essay; thesis statement showing whether you are addressing causes or effects.
Body:	Listing of various causes or effects. Select the most important ones. Use a topic sentence for each paragraph. Support each general statement with details and examples.
Conclusion:	Short paragraph suggesting a possible solution or prediction.

Suggested Topics:

Causes/effects of a particular business trend, e.g. foreign investment
Causes/effects of a particular societal change, e.g. career women in your culture
Reasons for choosing a particular career
Causes/effects of misunderstandings between people of different cultures
Causes/effects of a problem in your native country, e.g. bribery
Causes (or effects) of an important decision you have made in your life

Some advice:

Please do not try to write about broad social problems or medical problems unless you have some expertise in the field. You will not be able to write an essay about "The Effects of Smoking", for example, and make it specific, interesting, and original unless you have already done some in-depth study of the subject. Topics to avoid are the causes or effects of the following:

divorce	the homeless	drinking and driving
smoking	violent crime in America	alcoholism
T.V. violence	teenage pregnancy	the budget deficit

ENL 262: UPPER ADVANCED WRITING   Name: _____

Peer Review: Cause /Effect essay

Writer: _____

Title: _____

1. Write the thesis statement of the essay.

2. What is the topic of each body paragraph?

    A.

    B.

    C.

3. Are there details and examples in each body paragraph?

4. What is the best part of this essay? Why?

5. How do you think the writer could improve this essay? Give one suggestion about how he/she can improve the essay.

6. On the back of this sheet, write a one-paragraph response to the essay.

Cause essay

Economic Crisis as a Cause of Poverty in Russia

In the 1960's, the Soviet leader Nikita Khrushchov predicted that Russia would change dramatically in twenty years. "Our children will continue to live in COMMUNISM!" People were inspired and started working hard trying to achieve the "bright future". But it did not work out exactly as predicted. Now we have seen the start of the transformation of Russia, but not under the Communist control suggested by the First Secretary. Russia rapidly changed from a socialist system of government to an elected form of democracy. Yeltsin's cabinet has come to power. As these political changes occurred, there was also a shift in the economic field to a market economy. I voted for Boris Yeltsin to be president. In my opinion, the steps he took were the right ones. And I still support Russia's President. But the fact is that this fundamental turn in economic form has produced an unprecedented degree of poverty in Russia. The process of economic change is not complete, and the level of poverty has risen so high that the Russian government now reports that more than 70% of the Russian people live in poverty. While many factors contribute to poverty, three of the most important in the context of great economic changes are low productivity, inflation, and crime.

The Russian people never had the right to own a private business. Now they have such a right, yet they don't have any capital. Moreover, people do not want to start their own business. Why? - It's not beneficial. The government continues to overtax success and overreward failure and losing businesses. There is a good example. Three years ago, my father, Ibrahim Gadjiev, who is a doctor in Kursk, Russia, decided to run his own business. It was not easy because of the absence of clear laws, but there were skills, desire, and hope. He came to Portland last August and, of course, had to answer a lot of my questions about the situation in Russia. The information that today's tax is 85% made me upset. Concerning my father, it means he has to spend almost the whole income on staff salaries; he cannot afford to acquire better equipment, which is now more expensive in Russia than in the U.S.; he has to raise the prices for his services. Would you take the risk of an owner in Russia knowing this? What other way would you find to accumulate capital? Some Russians, mostly people from twenty to forty years old, have found the solution, which is now one part of the problem we will consider next: low productivity.

So what is the solution? - The easist one is retail selling. Not producing, but selling the products such as food, clothing, shoes, radio and TV equipment which are supplied from abroad. They call themselves "young businessmen", which is absolutely wrong, for almost none of them knows even the basics of economics. Nevertheless, this kind of "business" brings them a lot of money and leads to a huge gap between the very rich and everyone else. The other part of the low production problem is more serious. The result of the previous economic devotion to military goods has left the country with plants and factories which are not equipped to produce goods for the civilian population and trade. The factories now have no orders for military production, and this leads to the loss of jobs and low productivity.

The simple fact of poor production and lack of goods for the population is extreme inflation which has been in excess of 200% per year, according to the New York Times and other Western sources (1993). Even though now it is estimated at 7.7% per year (CNN News, October10, 1994), that figure is not reliable because of the day-to-day changes that seriously distort record-keeping. The October 11, 1994, issue of The Oregonian reports that the recent changes in the ruble's value against the dollar caused the government to raise prices for basic goods such as oil and gas 17% in one day. Frederick T. Smith, who is an attorney in Portland and also the president of a Russian-American trading company called"AMERUSS" states: "Inflation is making it impossible to do normal business with Russians. For example, prices agreed upon today will be outdated within one week because of rapid inflation. If you buy material today, by the time it is delivered, inflation will have made the price of the goods too high to complete the transaction." It is really a big risk for foreign companies to do business in Russia today.

All these problems are very complicated, but in my opinion, the most dangerous one is crime. Crime has contributed to pushing large numbers of people into poverty. The issue of crime as a cause of inflation is simple to understand. If goods are stolen or protection money is paid to criminals, those costs for the lost goods or extra amounts paid must be recovered by raising prices, which is inflation by definition. And it also harms foreign investment.

We can clearly see how tightly these problems are related. No doubt Russia is ill. As we know, there are two solutions for illness: recovery or death. The medicines for Russia's economic illness are well known in the West. How long it will take to get Russia to take its medicine remains to be seen.

Ella Gadjieva

Effect essay

The Effects of Urbanization in Ecuador

Ecuador is a small Andean country of around twelve million people. During the past twenty years, the population has increased considerably in Quito and Guayaquil, which are the most important urban areas in the country. Overpopulation in these cities aggravates many problems that already existed. Many farmers and their families who moved to the city live in deplorable housing conditions in the marginal areas around the cities. This uncontrolled immigration has affected the social dynamic of the families that live in these crowded conditions.

Farmworkers started to abandon their land and move to the cities in the era of "The Petroleum Boom" in the 1970's. With the discovery of this mineral resource, the country experienced a period of economic prosperity, while agriculture was neglected. Farmers did not receive the necessary services to perform their daily activities appropriately. Health services, education, and other government services were not easily accessible because long distances existed betweeen farms and the closest important towns. Despite these difficulties, farmers did not lack food or a relatively comfortable place to live. However, they moved to the cities in the hope that they could find better jobs and an education for their children.

They did not find in the city what they expected. The country's bad administration, characterized by waste, disorganization, and illegal negotiatations, has led to an economic slump. Moreover, there was a real inability of the city government to shelter the hundreds of immigrants that were trying to settle there. Consequently, immigrants who have moved to the city found themselves forced to live in crowded spaces in marginal areas of the city. For example, six people or more live in a two or three room house. Many houses are occupied by two or even three families. The extended family is the dominant family structure in these areas. These areas are called "popular neighborhoods", and they do not have the basic infrastructure, such as sanitary water, electricity, and a drainage system.

We can find families with five or more children sharing two beds in one or two rooms. When the children grow up and get married, they are not able to live independently from their parents, and very often they stay at their parent's house. Lack of skills, work, and education are some of the reasons why young couples have to live with their parents. This not only affects the couple's relationship, but it also affects the family structure. It is almost impossible to define what the roles of the members are. Whose rules do the children follow: their grandparents' or their parents'? Very often the parents' opinions influence many decisions that the young couple make. Under those circumstances, the family lives in a constant state of dispute that sometimes ends in violence.

Crowded living conditions create serious problems that in extreme cases lead to domestic violence, incest, divorce, and child abuse. Immigration to the city does not improve the living conditions of the farmers; instead it only accentuates their poverty and its social consequences.

Thelma Vega

Discussion essay

A discussion essay explores both sides of an issue. The writer does not focus on his or her own opinions, as in an argument, but on the differing opinions of the opposing groups. A discussion essay may also review the advantages and disadvantages of a new idea.

Many news magazine articles are really discussions. Even though the author's preferences may show through, the point of the article is to outline the different arguments that both sides are making. Sometimes, the author of the article may show his or her preference in the concluding paragraph.

In a good discussion essay, the writer must present a <u>balanced</u> report of the <u>pros</u> and <u>cons</u>, or the <u>advantages</u> and <u>disadvantages</u>, of a particular issue. In the body paragraphs of the essay, the writer must avoid showing <u>bias</u>. The point of a good discussion essay is to allow the reader to make the choice once he or she has reviewed the balanced information given by the writer.

Organization   (at least 4 paragraphs)

1. Use an anecdote, set of statistics, etc. to illustrate the issue; include a thesis statement which indicates that you are going to discuss both sides of the issue.

2. Arguments <u>pro</u>, or advantages

3. Arguments <u>con</u>, or disadvantages

4. Conclusion: you may predict the outcome of the current debate, offer your own opinions at this point, or suggest a compromise that will solve the problem.

   Note: You could organize your essay so that the arguments <u>con</u> come before the arguments <u>pro</u>.

Vocabulary: transition words

on the other hand	first
conversely	initially
on the contrary	second
however	third
	finally

Discussion essay: topics

Choose a topic that you can write about in a very specific way. Don't try to explain one of the world's major issues in your discussion essay. It would be much more interesting if you could narrow a general topic to a particular time and place that you are very familiar with. For example, the topic of "birth control" could be narrowed to "Making birth control information available to Portland area high school students." Now, that would be an interesting topic to discuss. In addition, if you needed more information, you could interview people who may have opinions about this issue.

You may also discuss the advantages and disadvantages of an idea or proposal for your discussion essay. For example, you may want to write about the idea that ENNL classes should be Pass/No Pass rather than graded A to F. You would then discuss the advantages and disadvantages of this idea.

When choosing a topic, think of an issue or idea and then do some narrowing in one of the following ways:

   a. to a particular place (country, region, city, suburb, etc.)

   b. to a particular aspect of the issue (for example, "condoms" instead of "birth control")

   c. to a particular group that might be affected (e.g. high school students, senior citizens)

Suggested topics for discussion essay:

1. Dropping out of college in order to learn about "the real world"
2. Having a baby after the traditional childbearing years
3. Returning to one's native country to find a marriage partner
4. Requiring foreign language proficiency for high school graduation in Oregon
5. Having women serve in combat in the military
6. Providing nursing home care for an elderly relative
7. Requiring young women under 18 to have a parent's permission in order to receive an abortion
8. Allowing only the English language as the medium of instruction in U.S. schools
9. Using cellular phones while driving
10. Using force in response to terrorism
11. Requiring welfare recipients to work while receiving benefits
12. Placing prisons in population centers

13. Allowing sex offenders to return to their communities without warning neighbors
14. Using marijuana for medicinal purposes
15. Arranging for older family members to immigrate to the U.S.
16. Having term limits for members of Congress
17. Moving out of one's parents' home before marriage
18. Providing educational and medical services to illegal immigrants
19. Teaching pre-school children two languages
20. Requiring engaged couples to have counseling before marriage
21. Reducing the future number of legal immigrants permitted to enter the U.S
22. Seeking U.S. citizenship when it means giving up one's original citizenship
23. Wearing of school uniforms by elementary and secondary students
24. Raising the legal driving age in Oregon to 18
25. Allowing Native American tribes to resume whaling for cultural and/or subsistence reasons
26. Cloning human beings
27. Censorship of the Internet
28. Two choices for a four-year college
29. Sending a manned space mission to Mars
30. Selling your house on your own vs. using a real estate agent
31. Spanking young children
32. Requiring air bags on the passenger side of a car
33. Reducing the standard work week to 30 hours
34. Giving money to panhandlers
35. Using animals in laboratory experiments
36. Legalizing gambling in Oregon
37. Legalizing prostitution
38. Distance learning
39. Weight restrictions for certain jobs
40. Trading with countries which have "human rights" problems

Advice:

Please do not choose a 'hackneyed' topic for your discussion essay. 'Hackneyed' means 'completely ordinary' (and usually unexciting). Such topics include smoking, alcohol, abortion, the death penalty, and euthanasia. These topics have been written about so often in the past that it would be extremely difficult to come up with something fresh and interesting to say about them. Strive to be original!

ENL 262: UPPER ADVANCED WRITING   Name: _____

Peer Review: Discussion essay

Title: _____

Writer: _____

1. Write the thesis statement of the essay.

2. What kind of introduction does it have (anecdote, statistics, statement by expert, etc.?) Is the introduction interesting and effective? Why/why not?

3. List the arguments <u>pro</u> below:

4. List the arguments <u>con</u>:

5. Is the body of the essay well-balanced and free of bias?

6. What is the best part of the essay? Why?

7. What is the least effective part of the essay? Give a suggestion on how the writer could improve it.

8. Write a short paragraph in response to the essay.

Discussion essay

Should Mazatlan Continue Its Carnival?

For some people, a carnival means freedom to express all human emotions. For others, a carnival is a festival in which everything brings happiness, merriment, and cheerfulness. There are many carnivals around the world throughout the year. My hometown has had its own carnival for many years. Due to the fact that it is a prestigious event, people from many cities come to the town to take part in it. The beauty queen contest is the principal attraction. The folk music and the Mazatlan cuisine are other attractions that the carnival offers visitors. In the past few years, however, it has been a topic of controversy among the people of Mazatlan. Opinions are divided among the district's politicians, some of whom support it as an old tradition that should be celebrated forever, and others who think that the carnival has lost its authenticity, sense of tradition, and overall value.

Supporters argue that the carnival is a very old festival that has taken place for more than a hundred years. They feel it is a celebration that has characterized the city for many years and should not be suspended. They insist nobody has the right to take away a tradition that belongs to everyone in the city.

They also argue that the people's poor working conditions, salaries, and lack of recognition on the job have created a stressful and infuriating environment for them. They need to have incentives to work. That is, they need motivation and entertainment to encourage them to perform better. Supporters insist that the carnival is a way of getting away from problems and worries. Some people work very hard throughout the year just waiting for carnival. Some save their money to spend on their families during the five days of the carnival.

A third argument is that in the course of those days, the differences of social class are removed. Everyone has the same status. During the carnival, people gather together on a Sunday night to appreciate a big parade that takes place along the waterfront. Later, everybody goes to celebrate on the other side of the city, which is well-known as "Old Mazatlan". There, people share a beer, a smile, a dinner. Supporters say that these experiences are possible only once a year, and that nobody has the right to deprive the community of this enjoyment.

Finally, supporters say the economy in Mazatlan needs the revenue that this event generates for the city. The city's major industry is tourism, and the carnival is a good way to promote national and international tourism. They believe that suspending the carnival could harm the economy enormously, and they recommend aggressive marketing all over the world.

On the other hand, opponents have strong arguments too. They have three major reasons for no longer supporting the carnival. First, they consider that it has lost all of its real value. For instance, during carnival, the city receives many national visitors who often cause problems such as robberies, assaults, and other violent crimes. Opponents insist that the city lacks the security to protect the citizens and others during the carnival. To them, this celebration has come to mean nothing more than violence and crime.

A second argument of the opponents is the fact that people spend money they do not have. Households try to do anything possible to obtain money to spend during the carnival. Some borrow too much money to be able to afford the expenses of this special time. Opponents claim that people should pay more attention to a better living standards and a better educational system. They think that saving or borrowing money to spend during carnival is fruitless and in the long run will bring on more personal debt.

In addition, opponents believe that the city has many basic necessities to take care of. For example, providing sanitation programs, expanding access to clean drinking water, and providing better educational programs should take precedence over the carnival. They believe that because the city needs so many basic things, it is ridiculous to spend money on something as unproductive as the carnival. They say the government should think more about fighting poverty.

Both sides have points of view that are reasonable. If the carnival remains the same, it may be harmful for everyone in the town. However, the city needs the revenue that the carnival brings in. To find a good solution to this matter, it is necessary to analyze both sides and then consider the benefits and losses that any change can result in. One solution might be reducing the city's expenses for the carnival in order to save money. More aggressive promotion all over the world could raise higher revenue for the town. In this way, the city would have the ability to help those who need it. Perhaps improved coordination among the citizens could bring about a creative solution. The city government, the carnival organizers, and average citizens have to join forces to reach a resolution from which everyone would benefit.

Gabriela   Mann

Classification essay

Classification is the process of grouping together people or things that are alike in some way. A simple classification would be to classify cars in terms of their body size: full-size, mid-size, compacts, and sub-compacts, or Portland Community College in terms of its different campuses. These groups or categories, are helpful in letting you see relationships among people or objects. They help you to organize information and compare it.

However, these categories often do not exist in the real world; they may exist only in your mind. You create them using some criterion or organizing principle. For example, you can classify college students by looking at their study habits: those who schedule study time, those who cram before a test, and those who hardly study at all. The organizing principle for classifying students in the example above is the different ways that they study. On the other hand, you could just as easily have classified students according to their age, their grade point average, or their religion. You could just as easily have classified cars according to their cost, their gas mileage, or their body style.

If you want your categories to be clear and consistent when you create a classification, make sure that you follow these two rules:

1. Use only one criterion or organizing principle so that everyone or everything fits into only one category, for example:
   Group people according to income, or intelligence, or industriousness-- but not according to income and intelligence, or intelligence and....

2. Create categories that allow room for everyone or everything you are classifying

Topic selection

Classification essays are commonly used in business, science, advertising, and editorials. However, at this level, a classification essay can be <u>subjective</u>. Sometimes classification essays are humorous or sarcastic. Choose a topic of interest to you and your audience. Use your imagination. Have fun, be creative, and be original -- the structure is straightforward.

You will have to write a <u>thesis statement</u> which you will then have to support in the details of the essay. An example of an appropriate thesis statement might be:

> **Girls have various ways of choosing boyfriends: for some, money is everything; for others, love conquers all; and for the last group, common interests and values are what is most important.**

The body of the essay should explore the qualities of each category, with clear examples and anecdotes.

Suggestions for topics:

People: husbands, wives, in-laws, teachers, students, friends, enemies, bosses, co-workers, doctors, nurses, patients, babies, ex-wives, ex-husbands, grandparents, teenagers, mothers, fathers, lawyers, secretaries, T.V. news announcers, hairstylists, book lovers, ice-cream eaters, umbrella users, disco dancers, market vendors, Beanie Baby collectors, etc.

Places: vacation spots, campgrounds, tutoring centers, college campuses, airports, freeways, back yards, front porches, parks, gardens, vegetable plots, video game arcades, movie theaters, Chinese restaurants, car washes, hiking trails, etc.

Habits: lunch habits, morning routines, test-taking, jogging, T.V. watching, bus riding, letter writing, dishwashing, house cleaning, house painting, playing, changing diapers, taking a shower, etc.

Occasions: weddings, funerals, birthday parties, Christmas celebrations, dinner parties, commencements, company meetings, family picnics, Mother's Day celebrations, etc.

Some advice:

1. At this level, don't choose topics that are already obvious to the reader. For example, don't write about the four levels of college students (freshmen, sophomores, juniors, and seniors) or the three branches of government (legislative, executive, judicial). You should try to be original and creative in your selection of a topic.

2. Remember that you should have a <u>rationale</u> for your categories. Think about your life experiences. Do you want to make a social comment or give advice? For example, imagine that you just got out of the hospital after a long stay. You noticed that there was a wide range in the quality of nursing care, so you decide to categorize nurses according to the way they treat their patients; or you have worked for various lawn service companies, so you are able to categorize them for the reader.

3. Make sure that your categories can be clearly labelled, for example: "helpful husbands, unhelpful husbands, and reluctant husbands" **NOT** "helpful husbands, unhelpful husbands, and the ones in the middle."

ENL 262: UPPER ADVANCED WRITING　　　　Name: _____

Classification Essay: Peer Review

Title: _____

Writer: _____

1. Write the thesis statement below. What are the categories the author is describing?

2. Does the writer give equal space to each category or group? If not, please comment.

3. Is each body paragraph developed with sufficient detail?

4. In your opinion, what is the best part of this essay, and why?

5. Which part of this essay is the least effective? How would you suggest that the writer change it?

6. On the back of this sheet, write a response to your classmate's classification essay.

Classification essay

Lithuanian Immigrants in the United States

About twenty years ago, when I lived in Lithuania, I met a young Lithuanian man who was born, raised and educated in the U.S. I remember that I was very impressed with his excellent knowledge of the Lithuanian language, culture and literature. At that time, there wasn't much information in my country about the preservation of the Lithuanian language and culture among emigrants. My meeting with that young man broadened my outlook in this area. However, I learned much more about this matter when I came to live here and became acquainted with many families of Lithuanian origin. I met people with different outlooks on the need to maintain the native language and culture abroad. Generally, the Lithuanian immigrants could be divided into three groups according to their approaches to the preservation of native language and culture.

The first group includes people who do not teach their children the Lithuanian language and culture. They want their children to be Americanized from the day they are born. Some of these people think that learning the native language may be a burden on their children and may inhibit their success in the American schools. As a consequence, parents in this group speak with their children only in English. Within this group there are families in which both parents speak both languages fluently and families in which parents speak only Lithuanian well but use their limited English to communicate with their children.

The second group of people consists of Lithuanians who teach their children only the native language and want their children to speak Lithuanian well before attending an American school. I recently became well acquainted with one such family. In this family, the parents never speak English with their children and they allow their children to watch only taped Lithuanian TV programs. In fact, they do not want their children to be exposed to the predominant American culture and language, feeling that enough exposure will come when the children go to public school. These families socialize as much as possible with other families whose children speak Lithuanian, and they often organize Lithuanian community gatherings with traditional ceremonies, festive food, dancing and music.

The third group includes the people who teach their children both English and Lithuanian. A majority of Lithuanian immigrants belong to this category. The families of my relatives represent these immigrants well. Their children attend American kindergarten and public school, and on Saturdays they take Lithuanian language and history classes in the Lithuanian Saturday School. The children participate in both American and Lithuanian community activities. Some parents enroll their children in the Lithuanian Vasario 16 School in Germany with the purpose of improving the children's native language. Young people from all over the world come there to study a high school program in the Lithuanian language. Recently, since Lithuania became independent, many immigrants have sent their children to summer schools in Lithuania where they study their parents' language and participate in cultural events.

Over the years, I have observed different approaches to the need for native language and culture preservation among Lithuanian immigrants in the U.S. Some of these immigrants see no need to preserve their past, some exert every effort to preserve it, even at the expense of becoming isolated in American society, and finally, some families choose to strike a delicate balance between the American culture of the present and the Lithuanian heritage of the past.

Margarita Vainiene

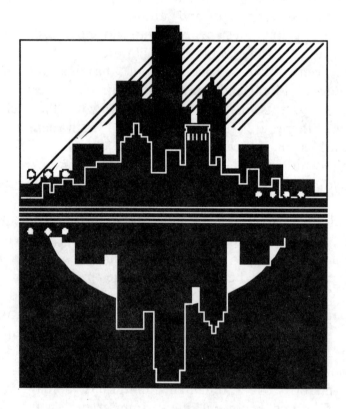

Problem/Solution Essay

A problem/solution essay presents a problem, usually discussing several aspects of the problem, then concludes by discussing solutions to the problem. The problem may be addressed in the following ways:

1. Effects only:	Describe the problem only in terms of its effects. Use examples.
2. Causes and effects -	In addition to the effects, outline the causes of the problem. This approach is especially appropriate when discussing solutions in terms of preventive measures.
3. Extended example -	After a topic sentence, illustrate the problem by using an extended example, e.g. tell the story of someone who experienced the problem, or continue the anecdote from your introduction.

The solutions may be presented in various ways and you have to think about which way would be the most appropriate for the particular problem you are discussing. Here are some ways to present solutions:

1. Preventive measures:	Ways to prevent the problem from occurring in the first place, such as how to prevent skin cancer.
2. A series of steps:	Suggest the easiest and most obvious solution first, but if that doesn't work, try something else, etc. For example, if you have a noisy neighbor, you might first talk to him/her; if that doesn't work, arrange for a mediator; etc. (a last resort might be to call the police).
3. Advice:	Give some advice and helpful hints.
4. A choice of solutions:	These solutions may be ones that have already been tried, including those which have been unsuccessful, and new solutions which you are proposing.

Make sure that your essay is well-balanced. The most original part of your essay, and the section which will require the most critical thinking, will be the solutions. Make sure that you address the solutions in depth. The solutions section of the essay should be as long or longer than the section describing the problem.

Suggestions for topics:

    Getting a baby to sleep
    Preventing a burglary of your house or apartment
    Preventing "burn-out" from work/study
    Dealing with stress
    Working and taking classes at the same time
    Raising children and working/taking classes
    Rationing TV time for your children
    Communicating effectively with your husband/wife/boss
    Finding the time to study
    Dealing with unwanted advances by a man/woman
    Making friends with Americans
    Making time for yourself
    Dealing with a noisy neighbor
    Caring for an elderly relative
    Using a credit card wisely
    Improving your G.P.A.
    Raising a child as a single parent
    Preventing teenage boys from joining gangs
    Speaking English intelligibly
    Keeping your house/apartment clean and tidy
    Preventing pipes from freezing in the winter
    Giving your children "quality time"
    Making sure that household members share chores equally
    Controlling dogs in your neighborhood
    Controlling speeding drivers in the suburbs
    Dealing with raccoons
    Managing the stress of divorce
    Coping with a heat wave
    Dealing with snow and ice
    Trying to prevent vandalism
    Finding ways to deal with co-workers you don't like
    Finding a fresh start after getting laid off
    Dealing with telephone solicitations
    Coping with a death in the family
    Working on pronouncing English intelligibly
    Dealing with relativesor friends who ask you for "favors" or money
    Breaking up with a girlfriend/boyfriend

ENL 262: UPPER ADVANCED WRITING   Name: _____

Problem/solution essay: Peer Review

Title: _____

Writer: _____

1. Write the thesis statement below.

2. Does the thesis statement mention the topic, the focus of the essay, and the idea that the author will address both the problem and solutions?

3. Does the writer begin the essay with an interesting anecdote or explanation? What is it about?

4. Is the essay well-balanced? Is there sufficient attention given to both the problem and possible solutions?

5. Is the conclusion effective? If not, how would you change it?

6. In your opinion, what is the best part of this essay, and why?

7. Which part of this essay is the least effective? How would you suggest that the writer change it?

8. Write a paragraph in response to your classmate's essay.

Problem/Solution essay

A Workaholic Husband and a Mean Wife

Most scientists are very busy with their research, so they don't have much free time to spend with their families or to do something fun for themselves. It's not good for them to spend too much time in the laboratory, but they do so anyway. Sometimes scientists become engrossed in their experiments, and they can't stop their work right in the middle of an experiment. They also need to go to their offices on weekends to check on their work. However, if the scientist is married, he or she is not the only one who suffers from this lifestyle. When a couple can't share their time, their commitment begins to weaken. I don't wish to exaggerate the problem, but I know some couples get divorced over the issue of job responsibilities. I appreciate the fact that some jobs are extremely demanding, but it's not acceptable for families to become victims of workaholism. My husband, who is a scientist, and I had to reach the point of crisis before we did something about this problem.

My husband is a biologist who works at O.H.S.U. as a researcher. Until recently, he often came home about dinner time, returned shortly afterward to the office, and then came home after midnight or in the early morning hours. This was not his daily schedule, but it happened frequently. Weekends were no exception because he went to the laboratory and worked at least two or three hours a day. I sometimes asked him to say exactly when he would come home, but he never kept his promises. He was always late. When I talked to a friend of mine, also a scientist's wife, she had the same complaint about her husband. I was furious with him, but at the same time, I worried about him driving his car late at night in a tired physical condition.

When I thought about it, I realized this whole issue is complicated by a cultural component. In other words, husbands and wives have different expectations of one another across cultures. In my native country, for example, most husbands come home very late because of their jobs and because their socialization with co-workers is expected. They often go to bars after work, and they go out without their wives on weekends to play golf, so many Japanese wives are accustomed to living almost without a husband. It's very sad. Some husbands come home late and have dinner at 10 or 11 o'clock and go to bed. They don't talk very much to their wives. We call this phenomenon "bath", "dinner", and "go to bed". That is, husbands don't talk to their wives except to use those words. I had thought that being married to an American and living in the United States, I would experience a different situation. How ironic!

After a thousand arguments about my husband's working schedule, I presented him with an ultimatum: "Me or your job?" He laughed at me. I know how stupid this question sounded, and I'm familiar with this kind of dialog from movies, TV, and novels. I was waiting for his reply, but he just sat there silently. Then I said, "Take your job, and work as hard and as long as you want to".

He was still mute. After a few minutes he asked me, "Then, what are you going to do?"

"I'll go back to Japan," I said. He seemed shocked. He didn't want me to do that, so we kept talking hour after hour to try to find a compromise. We talked so long that we had to take a dinner break in the process. Finally, we decided to make some rules that we both felt we could live with comfortably.

Rule one is that he has to come home by 6:30 p.m.; otherwise, he gets charged a dollar per minute, and that money goes into my personal account. If he comes home early, he gets credits that he can use for a number of things like back massages, special dinners, or the right to choose the video at Blockbuster. Second, he can return to the office twice a week after dinner, and he can work until noon on weekends as long as he agrees to take me somewhere like the theater or a restaurant during the remaining hours of the weekend. I've found that I sometimes have to be flexible about the weekend rules, but he has been abiding by all of the others quite well. More importantly, we're having a lot more fun together as a couple.

Now, after hours of deliberation and negotiation between the two of us, my husband realizes what I expect and I have accepted his love for his work. Our new arrangements are working quite well. I sympathize with him because he has a demanding wife, but in the long run, my way will enable me to enjoy my life with my partner. What's more, he'll probably enjoy his life more and live a little longer without his excessively workaholic ways.

Keiko Hejna

Extended Definition Essay

An extended definition essay explains both the scientific or dictionary meaning of something and the personal attitudes and emotions connected with it.

One interesting approach to this essay is to write about an event, idea, movement, symbol, personality, document, speech, policy, or organization that is associated with United States history or culture. You will need to give a factual definition of the topic, based on library research; a report about the attitudes and emotions associated with the topic, based on interviews with Americans; and, finally, your own analysis which synthesizes the "official definition," the attitudes of the people whom you interviewed, and your personal conclusions about the topic.

> The essay should be organized as follows:
>
> | | | |
> |---|---|---|
> | Part One: | **Denotation** | "Textbook" or encyclopedia definition |
> | Part Two: | **Connotation** | Report on interviews with at least two Americans about the topic |
> | Part Three: | **Synthesis** | An analysis of your own conclusions, based on what you have written in Parts One and Two. |

Although the essay is in three parts, it will be more than three paragraphs in length.

Your interviews with Americans should be carefully constructed: remember that you want to focus on attitudes, not information (which you can find in the library). Make sure that you interview people who have some knowledge about the topic and can give some interesting opinions about it. Try to choose two interviewees who may have different opinions about the topic, or different perspectives (for example, an older and a younger person, or a male and a female). Your interview questions should be based on the following:

> What does this term/topic/event mean to you?
> What is your opinion about his event?
> Why is it important to us? How has it affected our lives?
> How has it influenced our culture and history (in your opinion)?

PLEASE NOTE: Writing about a topic from U.S. history is only one way to approach the extended definition assignment. Your instructor may set another assignment, for example an interesting item in the news (Spice Girls, Pornography on the Internet, the Westside MAX line, the Beanie Babies craze, etc.)

Extended Definition essay - suggested topics

Places

Alcatraz
Three Mile Island
Ellis Island
The Dust Bowl
The Alamo
Gettysburg
Angel Island
The Panama Canal

Symbols

The Stars and Stripes (U.S. flag)
The Confederate Flag
Uncle Sam
The Bald Eagle

Ideas and Movements

Civil Disobedience
Prohibition
Homesteading
The Civil Rights Act
The Civil Rights Movement
The Black Power Movement
McCarthyism
Manifest Destiny
The New Deal
The Marshall Plan

Documents, Speeches, Policies

The Bill of Rights
The First Amendment
The U.S. Declaration of Independence
The Emancipation Proclamation
The "Star-Spangled Banner"
The Equal Rights Amendment
The Monroe Doctrine
The Stamp Act
The Sherman Anti-trust Act
NAFTA
Martin Luther King's "I Have a Dream" Speech
John F. Kennedy's "Ich Bin Ein Berliner" Speech
The Gettysburg Address
Nixon's "I am not a crook" speech

Events

The Lewis and Clark Expedition
Paul Revere's Ride
The Apollo 11 Moon Landing
The *Challenger* Disaster
D-Day
Watergate
Pearl Harbor
The Bay of Pigs
The Great Depression
Reconstruction
The Boston Tea Party
Wounded Knee
The Trail of Tears
The Underground Railroad
The Oregon Trail
The California Gold Rush
The Missouri Compromise
The Assassination of John F. Kennedy
The Spanish-American War
Kent State
The Internment of Japanese in World War II
The U.S. Attack on Libya
The Bombing of Pan-Am Flight 103
The Iran Hostage Crisis
The Gulf War
U.S. involvement in Somalia
U.S. involvement in Haiti
U.S. involvement in Nicaragua
U.S. troops in Bosnia
The Insider Trading Scandal
The Savings and Loans Crisis
The Dred Scott Decision
The Scopes Monkey Trial

Organizations

The Peace Corps
The American Indian Movement
The Mafia
The NAACP
The Hemlock Society
The Pony Express
Head Start
MADD
NARAL
Greenpeace

ENL 262: UPPER ADVANCED WRITING   Name: _____

Peer Review: Extended Definition essay

Title: _____

Writer: _____

1. Answer the following questions about the topic:

    Who?

    What?

    When?

    Where?

    How?

    Why?

2. Do you think that the factual information that the writer gives is complete and accurate? Is there anything more you want to know?

3. Are the reports of the interviews interesting? Are the interviewees' opinions and their reasons for their opinions stated clearly?

4. Does the writer give a detailed synthesis of the information?

5. What is the best part of this essay?

6. Give one area of the essay which could be improved.

7. Write a short response to your classmate's essay in complete sentences.

Extended Definition essay

The American Flag

"Flag - a piece of cloth, varying in size, shape, color, and design, usually attached at one end to a staff or cord, and used as the symbol of a nation, state, or organization as a means of signaling, etc. " (<u>The Random House Dictionary of the English Language</u>).

From June 14, 1777, when the Second Continental Congress adopted a design for the American flag, to July 4, 1959, when Hawaii entered the United States, the flag changed its look several times. The first flag had thirteen stripes, alternately red and white, and thirteen stars - white in a blue field, representing " a new constellation." Today's flag still has thirteen stripes representing the Union, and fifty stars in a blue field representing all states of the United States of America (Giblin, <u>Fireworks, Picnics, and Flags</u>, 30).

There were several moments in American history when the flag played a very special role. It was an inspiration during the Revolutionary War, a sign of faith during the Civil War, a symbol of being on the side of right during World War I and World War II, and a symbol of protest against the government's policies during the Vietnam War (Giblin, 32-33). And according to a couple of people I interviewed, it has always had a special meaning for Americans. It has been important not only during such events like wars but also in ordinary, everyday life.

My friend Beth, a 34 year-old American, has very good feelings about the American flag. It is a symbol of her country. She remembers many special moments from her childhood when the flag was really admired even by children. She remembers that when she was a schoolgirl, all the children, before starting a new day in school, used to say the Pledge of Allegiance. Even after so many years, she still remembers the words and the feelings that accompanied the utterance. The flag was folded in a special way. Today, unfortunately, people do not pay too much attention to this fact. The flag is not supposed to touch the ground. If it happens, the flag should be burned. However, she does not accept such incidents like burning the flag for artistic purposes, or to express oneself. It is not right. The flag displayed and the national anthem played before sport games have always made her feel proud and touched, especially when she was one of the competitors. She recalls July 1969. All the people were so affected when the metal flag was erected on the moon by U.S. astronauts. People could talk only about this event. They were the first nation on the moon. She has always displayed the flag on all legal holidays, but one day is especially important for her. It is Memorial Day, which honors all war veterans. The multitude of the small flags, one on every grave, including her grandfather's grave, give her a special and difficult to describe feeling. She knows the meaning of the flag's colors. The American flag means a lot to her.

Michael, a 27 year-old friend of mine, agrees with most of Beth's opinions. For him, the flag is a symbol of the revolution that ended in the free country. The look of the flag is not important for him. It is just a symbol. There could be different colors. Yet, the blue, red, and white, and that special design have been kept for so long, from the beginning. He also remembers the Pledge of Allegiance, the flag and the national anthem before sport games, and the landing on the moon. He was just a baby then, and his parents took a picture of him by the TV set, where the astronauts with the flag were shown. That day was a great holiday for his parents. He also recalls all the occasions when he displays the U.S. flag: Veteran's Day, Presidents' Day, Thanksgiving, Flag Day, the Fourth of July ... In his life, there is also a day that brings special memories. It is the day of the funeral of his grandfather, who was a World War II veteran. He remembers the U.S. flag put on top of the casket to honor his grandfather. He recalls also the that the flag was folded and handed to his grandmother. He does not think that burning the flag is the right thing to do. People who do this, should not get any attention from the press and TV

    The American flag has always influenced American' lives and emotions. It has also influenced artists. "Stars and Stripes Forever" - composed by Phillip Sousa, "The Star-Spangled Banner"- the national anthem and the best-known of all American patriotic songs, composed by Francis Scott Key, "You're a Grand Old Flag" - composed by George M. Cohan, were inspired by the flag, and as the last said: "From my earliest days I was impressed with the fact that I had been born under the Stars and Stripes. And that has a great deal to do with everything I have written." The colors of fireworks, and colors of Uncle Sam's clothes on Independence Day are also inspired by the flag. So, what is so special about this piece of colorful cloth? Many people could probably say that their flag represents the country, traditions, blood and hard work of the ancestors, the history, and the future. Certainly, people in Poland would agree with this. Our flag had a special meaning during wars and disturbances inside our country. I suppose that most Poles do not think that the flag should be burnt for any reason. Several months ago, I could say that Polish people, in contrast to Americans, have special feelings for the flag only during legal holidays, and later do not care about it. It was my feeling, and I was wrong. I changed my mind one rainy day when a strong wind tore off the Polish flag that was displayed by my American cousin's house. I felt pity for that piece of white and red cloth that was wet on the ground. It seemed so close to me then. I could not just walk by. I picked it up. Therefore, I think that emotions and feelings about flags are similar for many nations. We all feel that special warmth in our heart, and a thrill when our team wins and the flag is displayed, and the national anthem is played. We just do not realize and understand our feelings quite often. President Woodrow Wilson's words suggesting the "special thrill that Americans feel seeing the flag waving in the breeze on the Fourth of July" are certainly universal (Giblin 34). "This flag, which we honor, and under which we serve, is the emblem of our unity, our power, our thought, and our purpose as a nation."

Anna   Szczucka

Argument essay

An argument essay explores a controversial issue, one where various opinions may differ. In addition to describing the issue, you must try to get the reader to accept your point of view. You can do this by offering logical proof in a reasonable way. A good argument offers facts, examples, details, or statistics. These should either be well-known, or come from an authority on the topic. In some cases, you might support your argument with interviews. An argument involves critical thinking. Avoid fallacies and propaganda. Critical thinkers are well-informed about both sides of an issue. They can understand weaknesses in their own and their opponents' arguments and can also recognize points of compromise.

> **Organization**
>
> 1. Illustrate the issue using an anecdote, explanation, etc.; briefly explain both sides of the argument; include a thesis statement on the side which you defend.
>
> 2. Develop the argument by discussing and using verifiable evidence (use several paragraphs here).
>
> 3. Mention and refute counter arguments to the points you have discussed.
>
> 4. Reexamine your position and reevaluate its correctness. End with a warning, prediction, or value judgment.
>
> **Note:** It could be more useful to put the refutation <u>before</u> the paragraphs where you express your own point-of-view. Another organizational pattern in the body of the essay would be to use your own arguments to refute each of the opponents' arguments (point-counter-point).

Making a good argument

When writing an argument paper, some types of argument are more appropriate than others. For example, an argument needs to be free of bias, vagueness, and over-reliance on personal beliefs. In order to make your argument appealing and credible, use the following methods:

1. Testimonials: using the words of recognized experts to support your views.
2. Supported generalization: using facts, figures, and case studies to support a general statement.

3. Personal experience: relate the argument to your own experience or the experiences of people that you know.
4. Solid research and documentation from a variety of sources (different periodicals, interviews, etc.)
5. Careful refutation of the opponents' arguments, showing a balanced and fair consideration, not bias.

Examples of poor arguments:

1. Populist argument: stating that "everyone" thinks a certain way, or that "people" do things a certain way. Be more specific!

2. Stereotyping: for example, "All Americans are loud and rude"; "(certain nationalities) are lazy."

3. Threats: warning your audience of drastic consequences, e.g. "We will all be dead in 50 years if we don't take care of the ozone problem now."

4. Distortion: twisting arguments of your opponents in order to make your own argument stronger, e.g. "Pro-Choice supporters are really pro-death because they believe in abortion."

5. Personal attack: criticizing opponents directly rather than discussing the issues, e.g. "Mr. Travis Jones, leader of the animal rights movement, is an immoral fanatic who has been unfaithful to his wife 17 times in the last five years."

6. Slander: trying to persuade through emotional language rather than reason, e.g. "Gays are going to take over our society and schools unless we stop them."

7. Broad generalizations: making a sweeping statement without offering evidence, e.g. "ALL criminals come from broken homes."

8. Religious convictions: using your religious beliefs as proof. Not everyone will have the same beliefs as you do, and you need to convince a wider audience.

9. Poor reasoning: drawing conclusions that are not necessarily true or may be based on incomplete evidence, e.g. "I interviewed two Americans who were opposed to capital punishment; therefore, I conclude that the majority of Americans are opposed to capital punishment."

Refuting opposing arguments

In an essay where you give the opponents' arguments after you make your own arguments, you should give one or two of the opponents' strongest points. Usually, these points will focus on <u>different aspects of the issue</u> than the ones you have already given. When you <u>refute</u> the opponents' arguments, you don't have to prove that they are wrong. You can suggest that the arguments that they are focusing on are not as important as the arguments that you have raised, or you can allow some <u>concessions</u> and suggest some <u>compromises</u> that would still allow your case to be the stronger of the two.

The following is a sample outline of the pros and cons in an argument:

Topic: "At P.C.C., eating and drinking should be allowed during class."

Pros: 1. Some students don't have time to eat outside of class;

2. It allows for a more relaxed atmosphere, which helps students to learn;

3. It's a matter of individual freedom: allow eating and drinking as long as it doesn't interfere with the class.

Cons: 1. It can be messy; students in a following class may sit on some Coke that has been spilled on a seat, and the janitors complain about having to clean up too many spills.

Refutation: The janitors are paid to clean the classrooms; Messy students can be fined, or they can be told to clean up their own messes; most students are not messy.

2. It can be noisy: for example, someone eating potato chips; the the smell of food can also be distracting to other students.

Refutation: Most foods do not have strong smells; noisy eaters can be asked to stop, just like noisy talkers.

You will notice that the arguments *pro* focus on different aspects of the issue than the arguments *con*. The arguments *pro* need to be developed with strong, authoritative evidence and examples; you may make some concessions when you refute the arguments *con*, but don't make these arguments seem more attractive than your own.

Argument/discussion vocabulary

People:

proponents	opponents
supporters	detractors
defenders	
advocates	
pro-	anti-

Verbs:

believe	theorize	acknowledge	recognize
contend	fear	concede	realize
argue	estimate	admit	counter
claim	project	grant	disprove
assert	accept	rebut	advocate
refute	favor (be in favor of)		

Nouns:

belief
contention
claim
argument
conclusion
assertion

Adjectives:

inaccurate
incomplete
(in)valid
illogical
unproved

Transitions:

however
on the contrary (meaning: that isn't true)
conversely
on the other hand
despite this (fact)
in spite of (this)
although
while
actually
furthermore
in addition
nevertheless
therefore
thus

Topics

Choose your topic very carefully. If you can find a subject that is interesting for you, you will enjoy writing your essay more and probably do a better job. Make sure that your topic isn't too broad. Your arguments should be comprehensive. Choosing a manageable topic will make it possible to stay within the three to five page range while still effectively presenting all the arguments necessary to persuade the reader.

Please feel free to argue a social or political situation in your country if you are able to obtain the necessary factual information. Some topics in the news include the following:

animal rights	minimum wage	genetic engineering
shortening the work week	legalized gambling	sex education in schools
jail reform	legalizing drugs	trade policies
giving money to panhandlers	English Only	legalized prostitution
space exploration	tax reform	mandatory retirement
birth control policies	recycling	old growth forests
the Internet in education	school budgets	curfews for teenagers
gay marriage	bilingual education	raising the minimum wage
saving the salmon	welfare reform	U.N. sanctions and embargoes
assisted suicide	politicians' sex lives	landmines
trade with China	NAFTA	assisting troubled economies

There is also a long list of possible topics in the section in this Handbook on the discussion essay (pages 37 - 38).

Of course, it is always a wise choice to pick an issue with which you have had some experience, such as education, parenting, neighborhood issues, or a controversial topic from your own country. Otherwise, you may have to do some time-consuming research to familiarize yourself with the topic.

In addition, it is always important to **narrow yout topic**. After choosing an issue, try to confine your opinions about it to a particular place, time, or country. Make sure that this is clear in your thesis statement.

Some advice:

The following topics have been written about so much that all of the arguments on both sides are already familiar to most readers. Please choose a topic that is not related to these subjects:

abortion	capital punishment/the death penalty
euthanasia	working mothers
smoking	alcohol/drinking and driving
gun control	sex and violence on T.V.

Exercise 8

Practice arguments for debate

After you choose your topic, it would be a good idea to debate the issue with a classmate or friend. This way, you can discover some of the objections to your point-of-view.

The following arguments fall under the general topic of "education". Find a group of three to five other people and divide the group in half. Choose one of the topics below and stage an informal debate. One half of the group will support the statement and the other half will oppose it. (It doesn't matter what your personal beliefs are: you must be able to argue for either viewpoint). Your debate will consist of arguments and counter-arguments (refutations).

1. High schools should be segregated by sex.

2. Public schools should have regularly-scheduled prayer sessions

3. The current grading system (A-F) should be eliminated in favor of no grades, just C (completed) or I (incomplete).

4. People should pay higher taxes to maintain quality in public schools.

5. Class size at PCC should be kept at 15 students or fewer.

6. Attendance should not be part of the final grade in a college course.

7. An instructor's salary should depend upon the students' evaluation of his/her performance.

8. American high school students should wear uniforms.

9. American schools should begin the instruction of foreign languages at the elementary school level.

10. Each ENNL class should have an exit test which determines whether a student goes on to the next level or not.

ENL 262: UPPER ADVANCED WRITING Name: _____

Peer Review: Argument essay

Title: _____

Writer: _____

1. Write the thesis statement of the essay.

2. What kind of introduction does it have (anecdote, statistics, statement by expert, etc.?)

3. Is the introduction interesting and effective? Why/why not?

4. How many different arguments does the author make?

    List the arguments below:

5. List the opponents' arguments that the author gives.

6. Is the refutation effective? Why/Why not?

7. Is the conclusion effective? Why/Why not?

8. What is the best part of the essay? Why?

9. What is the least effective part of the essay? Give a suggestion on how the writer could improve it.

10. Write a short paragraph in response to your classmate's essay.

Argument essay

Manny

    Have you ever heard the word "manny"? It is not money. It is not nanny. "Manny" is a combination of "man" and "nanny." It means a male nanny. What do you think of them? Would you want one to take care of your children, or would you say, "Absolutely no thank you"? These days, there are some male nannies in the U.S. They are not so common, but they exist. Male nannies certified by a nanny agency make quite good caregivers, and they know how important childcare is for our future. However, it is very tough for them to get jobs. First and foremost, the agencies are reluctant to accept them. They are usually treated nastily by the agencies during the interview process. In many instances, they are kicked out, or they astonish the agency officials at first sight. And then they are asked very personal questions such as, "Are you gay?", "Do you have a girl friend?" probing into their personal life. Second, many parents are hesitant to hire them for their children as a nanny. Do you think that all of this is justified? Isn't it biased? These questions should be considered today.

    I learned this word just last weekend. A television program about "Mannies" appeared while I was doing some household chores. The "Mannies" on the show came from all over the West Coast. Some looked tender, and others looked rather strong like football players. Actually, one of them was a former college football player. At first glance, I doubted whether they could look after children. Furthermore, I convinced myself that children might fear them and not want to be with them. For these reasons, I didn't pay much attention at first. But as I watched, I began to change my mind. The program showed how well these "mannies" could deal with children, how much they loved children, and how hard they worked. As I was watching the program, my mind changed to supporting "mannies" in the same way I would support a female nanny. For instance, one "manny" who worked with a five or six-year-old boy said: "This job is not easy; it's rather tough. I have to pick him up at school and take him to the dentist, swimming lessons, and other activities. Also, I play with him, study with him, and give him meals. I am almost his mother." At the end of the video about how he worked with the little boy, the child hugged him, kissed him, and said, "I love you."

    Among many female nannies, there are women who have an advantage simply because of their gender. They may not put their hearts into the job at all. In fact, we know some horror stories about female nannies involved in abduction and child abuse. We can't place our trust in them simply because they are women. We have to know their personalities before we put them in charge of our precious children. When we find out the sensibility for taking care of children in their personalities, we can trust them and leave our children under their care. In such cases, why can't you hire a "manny"? The difference of gender has nothing to do with looking after children. We have to throw away the old idea that a caregiver must be a female.

Are you still skeptical about a "manny"? You may be feeling that a man would be clumsy with children. You may think they don't know how to change diapers, provide milk or baby food, and how to deal with children's tempers without yelling. In films like <u>Kramer vs. Kramer</u> or <u>Three Men and a Baby</u> men always seem to struggle with how to take care of children. Nevertheless, do these things happen only to men? I think these are also problems for women who become mothers for the first time. Caring for children is not genetically programmed. It takes practice after some struggles. Do you think you are convinced? Probably the concept of "manny" is so new for us. We may not be able to get used to it yet. We, however, have male nurses. They are not only working at war time any more but also working in may hospitals. According to the American Association of Colleges of Nursing, the number of male nursing students has been increasing recently (<u>Nation's Health</u>, Vol.2: 1994, P4). Today many patients are being treated by a male nurse. Why can't we praise the ability of a "manny"?

Hiring a nanny is a difficult decision for many parents and costs so much. Therefore, I want to ask you to see nanny candidates very carefully without prejudice towards men. What we have to consider is what is best for our children and who has the most wonderful personality. We already know about discrimination against women in the job market. Many women are still struggling. All women think that such discrimination should be done away with, and their ability should be appreciated. Therefore, women should be the first to approach this issue from the standpoint of fairness. We have to judge a "manny" based on ability. Couldn't you hire Mrs. Doubtfire?

Mari   Tokumitsu

IN-CLASS WRITING

Purpose of In-class Writing

The Upper Advanced Writing curriculum requires that you write at least three in-class essay tests during the quarter. One of these should be on the final examination. Students need to get a 'C' average on the in-class writing tests in order to pass the class. If students do not pass the in-class essay section of the final exam, they may fail the class.

The purpose of in-class writing is to test the student's real writing ability under examination conditions. Students will not know the essay questions before the in-class test. They should apply all they have learned in terms of essay development, organization, the thesis statement, syntax, and grammar. In the evaluation of in-class writing, particular attention will be paid to correct sentence structure. Students who are still making grammatical errors in every sentence will not pass an in-class writing test.

In-class essays will be hand-written on lined paper. Please write double-spaced - this makes it easier for the instructor to read and comment on your writing. You will usually be given 50 minutes to complete an in-class essay test. You will not be allowed to continue writing after the class period has ended.

Some students get very nervous during in-class writing tests. Ideas seem to vanish as soon as they get in the classroom, and they forget simple grammar rules. They are not alone! If you get nervous, use your time wisely at the beginning of the period. Write down your ideas in an organized outline. If you have a choice of topics, pay special attention to topic selection. Choose a topic which you can easily write about for at least 30 minutes without stopping. Focus on the organization of your essay and your basic sentence sentence structure. **You will not be allowed to bring in notes to your in-class writing test**.

Preparation

Here are some suggestions for in-class writing.

1. Spend at least 10 minutes at the beginning writing an outline of the following: a clear introduction with thesis statement; topic sentences and examples for a limited number of body paragraphs; a brief conclusion. See the sample essay outline on page 4 of this Handbook.

2. 30 minutes writing the essay. Don't write too much: the basic requirements for a good in-class essay will be logical development of ideas, clear organization, and sound sentence structure and punctuation.

3. Revise and edit for the final 10 minutes of class. Review for errors in usage of articles, verb tenses, verb forms, subject-verb agreement, prepositions, noun plurals, word forms, vocabulary, punctuation, and spelling. You may even have time to rewrite the essay.

Remember that the body paragraphs of your in-class essay should form the bulk of your writing. These should contain interesting details, explanations, and examples to illustrate your topic sentence. It is not the number of paragraphs, but rather how well they are developed which is important.

Reading response

Some writing assignments, including in-class writing assignments, may require you to 'respond' to an assigned reading. Of course, you will need to spend some time reading the assignment and making sure that you understand it fully before you respond to it. The most important part of the reading response is your thesis statement, in which you have to present an original idea based on the ideas in the reading.

Instructors will usually give you a question, or a set of questions to choose from, based on the reading. You will not know these questions before you take an in-class writing test. Make sure that your thesis statement conforms to the question that you have chosen to answer.

An essay question based on a reading may take one of the following forms, or a combination thereof:

a. disagreement with the author point by point

b. agreement with the author point by point

c. <u>pros</u> and <u>cons</u> of the issue (discussion)

d. <u>your</u> views on the issue (argument)

e. comparison or contrast with a similar situation

f. relationship of the issue to your own experience

g. expansion of the topic to include your own details and examples

h. an extended example of someone or something influenced by the issue

A reading response can be based on the following outline:

Part 1:	a. Summary of the author's main idea(s) <u>in your own words</u>. Use two to five sentences. Be brief! b. Thesis statement (<u>your</u> main idea). Use one sentence. Example: "Alison Sprout asserts that U.S. students are outperformed by students in many other countries. She thinks that the U.S. educational system may not challenge students enough. I believe that U.S. high schools should raise their academic standards and make the students more accountable.
Part 2:	Respond to the article in your own words. Each paragraph should have a topic sentence. Use transition words. This will be the lengthiest part of your essay. You have already briefly summarized the article, so don't repeat ideas from the reading in detail. In this part of the essay, you should be focusing on your own ideas and supporting your thesis statement.
Part 3:	A brief conclusion in which you synthesize the points made by the author of the reading and your own ideas.

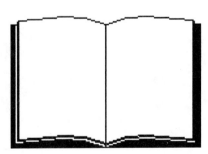

Exercise 9

Read the article "Are American Schools Too Easy?", by Albert Shanker, on pages 91-92 of this Handbook. Choose <u>one</u> of the following questions and write a reading response essay. Fill out the outline on this page before you write.

> 1. Do you have a national curriculum in your country? What are the advantages and disadvantages of your country's national curriculum?
>
> 2. Do you agree with Albert Shanker that some American teachers "... don't ask enough of students"? Explain your answer using examples.
>
> 3. Is Albert Shanker being reasonable when he compares the study of English or math to "... preparing for the Olympics"?

Outline

Introductory paragraph
1. Summary of article contents:

2. Thesis statement:

Body paragraphs
Major points (List by number; sketch out some details and examples):

Concluding paragraph

THE RESEARCH PAPER

Purpose of the Research Paper

The final paper in Upper Advanced Writing is one in which you include ideas from other people's speech or writing. Since you did not originate these ideas, you must acknowledge them with proper documentation. This short research paper should be at least five pages long, not including the list of works cited, and typed double-spaced.

You will begin your research by going to the **library**. There, you will search for the information that you need. Find sources that fit your topic and **take notes**. You may then use these notes (from readings, interviews, T.V. documentaries, etc.) as sources for the specific points that you make in your research paper.

Source information can be presented in three ways: by **quoting** the exact words from a source; by **paraphrasing** a statement in your own words; or by **summarizing** another author's ideas, whether they be from a single paragraph or an entire article.

Whichever method you use to present another author's ideas, you must **document** the source so that the **reader** knows where you found the information.

The purpose of the research paper is to familiarize students with the basic conventions of college writing. You may be asked to write research papers in many different subject areas. In addition, students must become familiar with the conventions surrounding other people's original ideas. Never use another person's original idea without also citing his or her name and the source publication. If you use other people's ideas without citing your sources, you are **plagiarizing**.

Remember also that in any paper you write, **your** ideas are the most important. Good research is the basis and support for your own original ideas. A good research paper is not simply a collection of other people's ideas, in the form of quotes and summaries, that are brought together in one paper. You need to devote most of your research paper to the development of your own ideas, which must be based on your thesis statement.

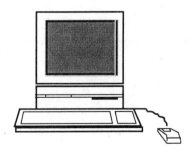

Plagiarism

Plagiarism is the act of using another writer's words or ideas without documenting the source of the information. <u>Webster's New Collegiate Dictionary</u> defines the verb 'plagiarize' as follows:

" TO STEAL AND PASS OFF (THE IDEAS AND WORDS OF ANOTHER) AS ONE'S OWN."

Plagiarizing, in other words, is seen as an act of **theft**. A plagiarizer **robs** another author of his or her ideas when he or she does not give that author credit.

Colleges and universities treat cases of plagiarism very seriously. A student who has been caught plagiarizing may fail the course, or even be expelled from the institution.

The key to avoiding plagiarism is good documentation of sources. Every time you use another author's ideas or words, use parenthetical documentation citing the author's name and the number of the page from which you got the information. In addition to showing your honesty, this documentation helps the reader to:

- a) find the sources of a writer's argument;
- b) do further reading on the subject by going back to the documented sources;
- c) understand the extent of the writer's research and the integrity of his or her approach.

The Learning Resource Center (LRC)

The library (Learning Resource Center) will be your primary source of information for the research paper. Periodicals, books, and the Worldwide Web will provide the sources that you can use to support your arguments in the paper. For a more detailed explanation of the LRC, see the ENNL Handbook for the Learning Resource Center. The reference librarians can help you with any problems that you may have in locating material. In addition, the LRC's How to . . . web page at <http://lrc.pcc.edu/pam/> has on-line tutorials for library research, Cat-A-Link, EbscoHost, the Worldwide Web, and web searches.

Periodicals: Periodicals (magazines, journals, newspapers) are kept on the periodical shelves in alphabetical order. To locate an article about a specific subject, you need to look in a periodical index under the subject heading of your choice. Periodicals can be checked out for one week.
> **EbscoHost** is an on-line computer database which catalogs thousands of periodicals. You may never have to go further than EbscoHost to get the information that you need since many periodical articles are stored in their complete form on the database. You may print out the articles on the library's computers, and EbscoHost may even be accessed using a home computer with a modem or Internet connection. EbscoHost is by far the most popular periodical index used by students.
> **The Reader's Guide to Periodical Literature** is a paper index that is updated regularly. It indexes all general interest English language magazines published in the United States.
> **The New York Times Index** is a series of volumes which index The New York Times newspaper. The newspaper is stored on microfilm or microfiche. Recent articles in the The New York Times are also stored on EbscoHost.

Books: Books are kept in three areas of the library: the checkout shelves, on reserve, or in the reference area. Books are classified acccording to the Dewey Decimal System of classification. Most books can be checked out for two weeks. Books on reserve have much shorter checkout periods. Reference books cannot be checked out.
> **Cat-A-Link** is the computerized card catalog which will help you to find the book that you need. You need to enter the book title, author, or subject in order to find what you are looking for.
> **The Reference Shelves** hold books and other items which you cannot check out of the library, including encyclopedias, dictionaries, manuals, directories, almanacs, government documents, and atlases.
> **CD-ROM references** that can be accessed on some computer terminals in the library include encyclopedias and atlases.

The Internet: Many computers at the library can access information that is on-line.
> **Netscape Navigator** is an Internet browser which is available on most computer terminals in the library. You can locate information by using a search engine (e.g. Lycos, Excite, or Yahoo) and typing in your topic.

Note-taking

Once you have selected a suitable topic, you need to collect information from outside sources to supply the facts and examples which will support your argument. Use the library to find material related to your topic.

When you have found a magazine article, encyclopedia entry, web page, or some other source related to your topic, you should read through it carefully and **take notes**. It is very important to take notes for several reasons: first, by taking notes in your own words, you will avoid **plagiarism**, or copying directly from the source; second, taking notes will allow you to save only the information which is directly related to your paper; third, taking notes will help you to become familiar with your source material.

You should establish a system for taking notes when you are doing research. Develop your own set of abbreviations and symbols so that you can take notes at speed. Write down only the most important words: nouns, verbs, statistics, names of people, places, dates. Function words like prepositions and articles are usually not noted down. Don't write complete sentences unless you are thinking of using the material for a direct quote (In this case, you should note the page number of the quote as well.).

On the next page, you can see a sample note-taking sheet. It includes space for bibliographical information which needs to be supplied at the end of your research paper.

Exercise 10

Write quick notes for the following sentences.

> Examples: "The second suggestion is to prevent T.V. from becoming an addiction."
>
> *Sugg. #2: prev. TV addiction*

1. "On the negative side, there is evidence that portrayals of violence on T.V. tend to stimulate aggressive behavior."

2. "In five- and six-year-olds, this can be expressed in a child's pushing, shoving, and striking other kids."

3. "The messages a first grader gets from *Mister Rogers' Neighborhood* are vastly different from those of, say, the *Geraldo* talk show."

4. "The first [suggestion] is to help your child become a wise television consumer."

Title of book or article: _____

Author(s): _____

Name of periodical: _____

Day or month of issue: _____

Page numbers: _____

Brief summary of contents in note form:

Quotes (give page number):

Below is a copy of a completed note-taking sheet for the article on the next page, "The Two Sides of Television," by Julius and Zelda Segal, Parents magazine, March 1990. *

Title of book or article: "The Two Sides of Television"

Author(s):   Julius & Zelda Segal

Name of periodical: Parents

Day or month of issue: March 1990

Page numbers: 186

Brief summary of contents in note form:

   Effects of T.V. on children:

      Negative: a) viol. -----> aggress. behavior
                       b) reinfor. sex stereotypes
                       c) less read. time
                       d) -----> nightmares & anxiety
                       e) less time for friendships

      Positive: a) stims. good behav.
                        b) good source of info.

   Solutions for parents: 1. sel. progs. & watch w/child
                                      2. make rules for watching
                                      3. don't send child to TV just to get out of way

Quotes (give page number):

   "All children can use our help in learning to relate wisely to that electronic force, which, for better or worse, is here to stay" (186).

   "It makes a difference whether the child is an occasional T.V. watcher or a miniature 'couch potato'" (186).

* Copyright © 1990 Gruner + Jahr USA Publishing. Reprinted from Parents Magazine by permission.

The Two Sides of Television

BY JULIUS AND ZELDA SEGAL

■ What effect does television have on children?

In the decades since television first came into the American home, researchers have addressed that question - so vital to parents - in scores of studies. The results give TV decidedly mixed reviews.

Pluses and minuses. On the negative side, there is evidence that portrayals of violence on TV tend to stimulate aggressive behavior. In five- and six-year-olds, this can be expressed in a child's pushing, shoving, and striking other kids. Though the research evidence is not as strong, there is room for concern too, that TV watching can reinforce sexual stereotypes, rob the child of the time needed to learn to read, cause anxiety and nightmares, and stifle opportunities to form friendships.

On the positive side, however, TV can stimulate humane behavior as well. If children look at depictions of kindness, compassion, and generosity, they are more likely to behave in a friendly and generous way. Moreover, TV can be an effective source of worthwhile information.

Whether watching television turns out to be harmful or rewarding depends on both the content of the programs a child sees and the amount of time he spends in front of the tube. The messages a first grader gets from *Mister Rogers' Neighborhood* are vastly different from those of, say, the *Geraldo* talk show. And especially for a five- or six-year-old, it makes a difference whether the child is an occasional TV watcher or a miniature "couch potato," who has little time for anything but TV.

Given the power of TV, parents are wise to consider ways to harness it in their children's behalf. Most researchers who have studied the subject agree on two suggestions:

The first is to help your child become a wise television consumer. Go over the listings in advance to select appropriate programs. When you can, watch the programs with him, especially when their content is likely to raise issues that are puzzling or troubling. It helps to make random viewing a family no-no; everyone should have a specific program in mind before turning on the set.

Establish ground rules. The second suggestion is to prevent TV from becoming an addiction. In the view of psychologists Dorothy G. Singer, Ed.D., and Jerome L. Singer, Ph.D., codirectors of Yale University's Family Television Research and Consultation Center, in New Haven, Connecticut, it is helpful to set down ground rules, such as No TV before school, during meals, during daytime hours, or before homework is done. And don't suggest that the child "go watch TV" whenever you are feeling overwhelmed or need privacy.

The effects of television are not likely to be the same for every child. They depend on his temperament - for example, his level of anxiety or aggressive tendencies - and on what else may be going on in his life, both at home and in school. Clearly, all children can use our help in learning to relate wisely to that electronic force, which, for better or worse, is here to stay. ✪

Quoting

Quoting a source lends authority to your argument. It also shows that you have consulted other sources. Quotes appear between quotation marks (" . . . . . "), and are usually introduced by a statement which may include the author and perhaps the periodical name. A direct quotation may be introduced objectively, or reflect your agreement or disagreement with the author's opinion. Quotations are followed by a parenthetical reference which gives the last name of the author ,if not already given in the introduction to the quote, and the page number of the quotation.

Here are some examples of quotations:

1. Objective:

"According to Albert Shanker, "Learning to write well or be competent in math is a lot like preparing for the Olympics"" (5).

2. Agreeing with the author:

"Albert Shanker makes an important point when he writes: "Learning to write well or be competent in math is a lot like preparing for the Olympics"" (5).

3. Disagreeing with the author:

"Albert Shanker makes too general an assertion when he writes: "Learning to write well or be competent in math is a lot like preparing for the Olympics"" (5).

or:

"Albert Shanker oversimplifies when he states: "Learning to write well or be competent in math is a lot like preparing for the Olympics"" (5).

Punctuation in quotations

Short quotations should be preceded by a **comma** (,) or **colon** (:). The first word of a quotation is usually capitalized.

If you decide to leave some words out of an author's original statement, use ellipsis (. . .) to show that words have been left out, for example: "Learning to write well . . . is a lot like preparing for the Olympics" (Shanker 5).

Use brackets ([ ]) when you are substituting words in the quotation, for example: "In [the American] system, how much work students do in a given class is up for grabs" (Shanker 5).

Parenthetical documentation follows the quotation and comes before the period (if the quotation ends a sentence).

Here is another example of a quote using ellipsis and brackets:

Original text: "During the following stage children acquire the language to describe and define different groups. It is at this point that deep feelings and strong attitudes - both positive and negative - are often conveyed by parents and other significant adults."

Quote: "During the [second] stage children acquire the language to describe and define different groups. It is at this point that deep feelings and strong attitudes . . . are often conveyed by parents and other significant adults" (Katz 185).

Note : Quotations of more than about 75 words should be separated from the text by indenting the passage quoted by 10 spaces. The entire quote should be single-spaced. No quotation marks are needed, for example:

Albert Shanker, writing in <u>On Campus</u>, states:

> Learning to write well or be competent in math is a lot like preparing for the Olympics. Youngsters have to work hard and do more than they think they can. This can be unpleasant and even border on the painful, but it takes this kind of stretching to achieve high levels in any field. In the U.S., a teacher who pushes students to work hard is viewed as unreasonable or even mean. But where there are external standards, a teacher is more like a coach - someone who is helping prepare kids for the Olympics - than like someone who has odd, personal ideas about education (Shanker 5).

Paraphrasing

Paraphrasing is the restatement of a phrase, sentence, or several sentences, in your own words.

It is convenient to paraphrase when you want to reword an author's words to fit your own style of writing. It also allows you to vary the method of presenting source material, so that you don't have too many quotes in your paper. Most summaries are, in effect, a series of paraphrases.

When paraphrasing you should always keep the full meaning and tone of the passage. Don't add any new information, and don't leave essential information out. Always remember to give the author's name and page number after the paraphrase.

Paraphrasing is an excellent test of vocabulary skills and reading comprehension. Paraphrase when you are answering questions for reading comprehension, as well as when you are using source information for your papers.

Use the following methods to paraphrase:

1. Synonyms

You can substitute words for phrases, or phrases for words, or one word for another. **Always** make sure that you change the **form** of the sentence substantially.

Example:

Original: "There are jobs out there that pay substantial amounts of money to people who don't have college degrees."
Paraphrase: There are well-paid positions for those who haven't graduated from college (Pratt and Begnones 17).

2. Changing the parts of speech

You can change nouns to verbs, or adjectives to adverbs, etc.

Example:

Original: "The collapse of communism and the end of the Cold War will mean a radical revision of the international order."
Paraphrase: Since communism has collapsed and the Cold War has ended, the world order will be radically revised (Guerrero 193).

3. Changing the word order in a sentence

Word order can be altered by changing from active to passive, changing the positions of phrases, etc.

Example:

Original: "For the last generation or two, psychiatrists have vigorously explored the sexual lives of children, the different kinds of family lives of children, the emotional disturbances of family life."

Paraphrase: The sexual lives of children, the different kinds of family lives they have, and their emotional problems have been intensely investigated by psychiatrists during the past few decades (Kritz 79).

4. Combining sentences

This can be done especially when the sentences are short.

Example:

Original: "We need to take care of the homeless and the poor, and attack drugs and crime. We must clean up our environment, rebuild our highways, railroads and merchant fleet."

Paraphrase: Americans must address the problems of homelessness, poverty, drugs, crime, the environment, and also reconstruct the highway, rail, and shipping systems (Johnson 32).

5. Making long sentences short

Divide long sentences into shorter ones.

Example:

Original: "What has helped push tuition costs down, they say, has been the the increasing competitiveness among schools, a more cost-conscious national attitude and the widespread frustration with the standard practice of discounting prices through scholarships and other forms of aid, while keeping tuition high."

Paraphrase: Three reasons are given for the reduction in college tuition. First, there is more and more competition between colleges. Second, people are more aware of high costs. Third, people are frustrated with the colleges charging high tuition rates while they commonly offer scholarships and other kinds of financial aid (Applebome A1).

Exercise 11

Follow the patterns to help you paraphrase the <u>c</u> sentence in each set.

1. a. A recent study showed that listening to jazz causes baldness.
   b. According to a recent study, you may go bald if you listen to jazz.

   c. Smith's experiment showed that jogging caused craziness.

   d. _____ jogging may cause _____

2. a. When they reach adulthood, young smokers may become chain smokers.
   b. In adulthood, young smokers sometimes become chain smokers.

   c. When they become old, joggers may have foot problems.

   d. In old age _____

3. a. Although there is a big unemployment problem, nothing has been done by the government.
   b. In spite of the great unemployment problem, the government has done nothing.

   c. Although there is a crsis, nothing has been done by the administration.

   d. In spite of _____

4. a. For the most part, citizens believe that teachers are hard workers.
   b. Citizens generally believe that teachers work hard.

   c. For the most part, voters believe that politicians are good speakers.

   d. _____ are believed by voters

5. a. This kind of problem might be found anywhere.
   b. We can find problems like this anywhere.

c. That kind of citizen can be depended on.

d. _____

_____

6. a. An unemployed person has difficulty keeping up hope.
b. It is hard for a person who is unemployed to remain hopeful.

c. A retired person usually has no difficulty continuing an active life.

d. _____

_____

7. a. He is not strong enough to recover.
b. Can he recover? No. He is too weak.

c. The president is not popular enough to be reelected.

d. _____

_____

8. a. In the opinion of many experts, there are several problems which can result from watching too much television, including the ideas that T.V. shows can contribute to the forming of sex stereotypes, watching violence on T.V. may lead to similarly violent behavior, T.V. watching takes times away from play and reading, and frightening shows may cause nightmares.
b. Experts note that T.V. watching may cause several problems. First, sex stereotypes may be formed from certain ideas on T.V. shows. Second, violent behavior may result from watching violence on T.V. Third, play and reading time may be diminished by watching T.V. Fourth, nightmares may be caused by watching frightening shows.
c. Before calling the police, you can go through several steps in dealing with a problem neighbor, for example you can try to talk to the neighbor and listen to his or her side of the story, or you can contact your Neighborhood Mediation Office, or you can get you Neighborhood Association to write the neighbor a letter.

d. _____

_____

Summarizing

In a paraphrase, a writer expresses another author's exact ideas using different words; however, in a summary the writer must decide which material to use and which to leave out. Most summaries make a passage shorter by keeping only the main ideas. You can summarize a paragraph, an article, or even an entire book.

The steps to be followed in summarizing a passage:

1. Understand clearly the content and organization of the passage.

2. Find the main idea. Sometimes, a paraphrase of the main idea is sufficient to convey the author's meaning.

3. If more than a paraphrase of the topic sentence is needed, look at the organization of the passage and take notes based on an outline:

    I. Main idea (thesis)

    II. Aspects of main idea

    III. Author's conclusions

4. Don't include examples unless they are necessary to an understanding of the author's idea.

5. Write your summary using only the outline you have made. **Don't look at the original article,** or you may find yourself copying word for word.

6. If you wish, begin your summary with a reference to the author, followed by the author's thesis. Use the present tense when introducing an author's statement, for example:

    Smith states that . . .
    Smith points out that . . .
    Robert Smith concludes that . . .
    According to Robert Smith, . . .

7. Remember to give a parenthetical reference after your summary.

Example of a summary:

The following are notes written from the article "The Two Sides of Television", by Julius and Zelda Segal, which appears on page 81 of this Handbook.

> *Effects of T.V. on children:*
>
> *Negative:*
>   a) viol. -----> aggress. behavior
>   b) reinfor. sex stereotypes
>   c) less read. time
>   d) -----> nightmares & anxiety
>   e) less time for friendhsips
>
> *Positive:*
>   a) stims. good behav.
>   b) good source of info.
>
> *Solutions for parents:*
>   1. sel. progs. & watch w/child
>   2. make rules for watching
>   3. don't send child to TV just to get out of way

Here is a possible summary of the article:

> According to Julius and Zelda Segal, watching too much television can have several negative effects on children. First, watching violence on T.V. can cause aggressive behavior. Second, watching T.V. may reinforce sex stereotypes. Third, children who watch a lot of T.V. may spend less time reading. In addition, T.V. shows may cause nightmares and anxiety. Finally, there is less time for friendships.
>
> The Segals also note some positive aspects of T.V. viewing, including the ideas that some shows may stimulate good behavior and that many shows are good sources of information.
>
> The Segals have three possible solutions for worried parents: they can select programs and then watch them with the child; they can establish rules for watching T.V.; and they should avoid sending the child to the T.V. just to get him or her out of their way (186).

Exercise 12

Read the article "Are American schools too easy?"* on the following pages. Try to make an outline of the passage. Use the plan below to help you. Some of the ideas have already been provided.

   I.   (Introduction)
        A.   Anecdote: _____

        _____

        B. Definition (thesis): <u>Why do students in other countries work harder than</u>

        <u>American   students?</u>_____

   II. (Body)
        A.   Cause: _____

        _____

        B. Effects of no national curriculum:
             1. _____
             2. _____
             3. _____
             4. _____

        C. Effects of having national curriculum: _____

        _____

   III. (Conclusion)
        _____
        _____

Exercise 13

Now try to write a brief summary of the article from your notes. Remember that you can choose the points you wish to emphasize in your summary.

* Copyright 1993, American Federation of Teachers. All rights reserved. Reprinted by permission.

Are American Schools Too Easy?

By Albert Shanker

Recently I saw a TV interview with some Russian youngsters who now live in the U.S. After some standard questions, the interviewer asked them to compare their school experiences here with their experiences in Russia. Every one of these seventh and eighth graders had the same response: They'd already learned the material they were getting in our seventh- and eighth-grade classes when they were in third or fourth grade in Russia. They said that school in the U.S. was very easy.

There was nothing unusual about this exchange. Indeed, most people who have met foreign students from France or Germany or Japan have heard the same things. And if we question students like these a little further, we find that they are far ahead of their U.S. counterparts because they are assigned more work and more challenging work, and they work harder to get it all done. But why do they work harder? They have the same distractions as American kids. They have TV sets and pop culture.

One of the main reasons is that these other countries have national curriculums. They have decided what students need to know and be able to do by the time they graduate from secondary school. And they've worked back from these goals to figure out what children should learn by the time they are ages 14 and 9.

That's not true in the U.S. Our 50 state governments have developed curriculum materials, but they are very broadly defined. So each school or teacher can select from this broad array and develop what amounts to an individual curriculum.

This makes for plenty of variety but very little continuity. As a result, students who move from one school - or even one class - to another often find they are out of sync because they have not studied the math or history on which the coming year's work will be based. In countries where there is a national curriculum, fewer students are lost - and fewer teachers are lost because they know what the students who walk into their classroom have already studied.

A national curriculum gives everyone involved - students, parents and teachers - a different perspective on schoolwork. In the U.S., when a teacher piles on the work, students are likely to object. They say it's too hard and too much, and they complain that other teachers or other schools don't expect that kind of work. Often parents support these objections. So there is a process of negotiation about schoolwork in which students, and frequently parents, play a big role.

Sometimes teachers don't ask enough of students. They feel sorry for some youngsters because of their socioeconomic or racial or ethnic background and decide they won't be able to do real work. So they teach a watered-down curriculum and shortchange youngsters who could learn if they were given a chance.

In our system, how much work students do in a given class is up for grabs. Sometimes it's determined by the willingness or resistance of students and parents. Sometimes it's based on the teacher's expectations. In any case, the level and amount of work common in countries with national curriculums is practically never reached here. The choices our system allows inevitably lead to softer standards and less work just as the mandates in other countries lead to more work and much higher levels of achievement. If a student or a parent in one of these countries does complain, the teacher says, "All the other third-grade youngsters are doing this work, and you can, too." And the teacher probably reminds the parents and child that falling behind now can lead to serious consequences later - like not passing an important exam.

Learning to write well or be competent in math is a lot like preparing for the Olympics. Youngsters have to work hard and do more than they think they can. This can be unpleasant and even border on the painful, but it takes this kind of stretching to achieve high levels in any field. In the U.S., a teacher who pushes students to work hard is viewed as unreasonable or even mean. But where there are external standards, a teacher is more like a coach - someone who is helping prepare kids for the Olympics - than like someone who has odd, personal ideas about education.

With a national curriculum, everybody knows what is required. If there also are clear and visible stakes - getting into university or an apprenticeship program - the pressure is on to make sure youngsters meet the standards. Without national standards and a national curriculum, there are no such pressures. That's why students in other countries work hard and do so well - and why students in our "easy" and undemanding schools do not. Knowing that should lead us to act.

Documentation

Whenever you quote, paraphrase, or summarize from a source such as a newspaper article, magazine article, encyclopedia entry, microfiche card, or book, you must **document your source** so that the reader knows where you found your information.

Documentation usually consists of putting the author's name and the page number of the information you are repeating in parentheses after your quotation, paraphrase, or summary.

If you have already mentioned the author's name before you give the information, then you only need to supply the page number of the quote.

You do not need to supply the name of the magazine, date, or publisher. The reader can discover this information when he or she turns to the list of **works cited** at the end of your paper.

Note : Some instructors may require different forms of documentation, such as footnotes, and different fields of study may use different conventions for documentation. Ask your instructor to explain which system he or she uses.

Here are some examples of documentation:

1. **Quote:** Malcolm W. Browne, writing about the population increase in Vietnam, states: " . . . unless the nation can change direction, the Vietnamese will face a catastrophe" (A5).

2. **Paraphrase:** The feminist movement's principal message was that women don't need men (Ebeling 9).

Note : When quoting or paraphrasing from a personal interview, it is not necessary to document the interviewee's name if it has already been mentioned in the text. The interviewee's full name, and the date of the interview, will appear in the list of works cited.

Special Punctuation Notes

1. Names of books and periodicals should be underlined, for example:
   <u>To Kill a Mockingbird</u>
   <u>Encyclopedia Americana</u>
   <u>Memory, Meaning, & Method</u>
   <u>National Geographic</u>
   <u>McCall's</u>
   <u>U.S. News & World Report</u>
   <u>The Oregonian</u>
   <u>The Wall Street Journal</u>

2. Names of articles should be put in quotations, for example:
   "Cooking Fish Southern Style"
   "The True Purpose of Education"
   "Using Your Home as an Investment"
   "Asian-American Population Explodes All Around U.S."

3. Names of sacred writing are not underlined or put in quotation marks, for example:
   the Bible
   the Koran
   the Talmud
   the Upanishads

4. Parenthetical documentation in the text always comes **before** the period, for example:
   "My child has watched cartoon shows such as He-Man and The Master of the Universe and G.I. Joe and his behavior is markedly more aggressive and violent after viewing these shows" (Glamour 89).

   "Many people would give anything to have a clone, mostly from fear of dying" (Walton 3).

   "Our research also suggests that difficulties in turning down one's emotions after a stressful event may be a major factor leading to adolescent mood disorders" (Dahl 18)

5. Articles, web pages, etc. without an author indicated should be cited using the title of the article, or the key words in the title, for example:
   "The family-friendly policies introduced by some companies with much fanfare - job sharing, flexible hours and the like - often don't hold up in practice" ("The Myth of Quality Time" 67).

Illustrations

It is always useful to illustrate your paper. This can be done in two ways: by using **tables** or **figures**. Only use illustrations if you also refer to them in your writing, for example: "Prison incarceration rates in Texas are the highest in the nation (see Table 1)."

Do not include a table or a figure in your paper if you are not going to refer to it in your text.

1. Tables

Tables show statistics. Make sure that each table in your paper is numbered (even if there is only one); the table should also have a title; the statistical information should be clearly presented; the full bibliographical information for the source should be given below the table.

Here is an example of a table:

Table 1

ENGLISH AS A NON-NATIVE LANGUAGE - Sylvania Campus
Students enrolled Fall 1993 - Fall 1995 by native country

Country	Fall 1993	Fall 1994	Fall 1995
	(as a percentage of total enrolled)		
China	2.9	4.3	6.3
Iran	2.4	3.1	4.1
Japan	8.8	3.1	6.7
Korea	4.4	3.5	4.1
Russia	4.7	3.9	4.1
Vietnam	53.7	55.0	36.6
Total number enrolled in ENNL at Sylvania Campus	339	256	268

Source: ENNL student records

2. Figures

A figure can be a graph, drawing, or even a photograph. All figures should be numbered, even if there is only one; be very careful to correctly label all parts of the figure if it is a graph; the title and source information are given **below** the figure.

Here is an example of a figure:

Figure 1. Traditional Yemeni dwelling, Ar-Rawdha, Yemen.

Note: If you obtained your picture or graph from another source, you must cite the source information when you give the information about the figure, for example:

Figure 4. U.S. Net National Savings as a Percentage of GNP, from <u>U.S. News and World Report</u>, 6 May 1991: 53.

The List of Works Cited

The list of works cited comes at the end of your research paper. It includes all the sources cited in your paper. These should be listed in alphabetical order, according to the author's last name. Sometimes an instructor may require a **bibliography**, which is a complete list of all the sources you have consulted, including those which are not cited in your paper.

Each type of source, such as a book, periodical, or encyclopedia, requires its own special way of being listed. Below are some examples of how you would list different types of sources. Please note that the second line of a listing is indented by six spaces.

1. **A book**

Wintle, Justin. <u>Romancing Vietnam: Inside the Boat Country</u>. New York: Pantheon, 1991.

2. **A book with two authors**

Denning, Keith and William R. Leben. <u>English Vocabulary Elements</u>. New York: Oxford University Press, 1995.

3. **An edited anthology**

Bender, David L., ed. <u>American Values: Opposing Viewpoints</u>. San Diego, CA: Greenhaven Press, 1989.

4. **An article in an anthology**

Cummings, Marlene A. "America Needs Multicultural Education in Its Schools," in <u>American Values: Opposing Viewpoints</u>, ed. David L. Bender. San Diego, CA: Greenhaven Press, 1989. 294-98.

5. **An article in a monthly magazine**

Mitchell, John G.. "Our Polluted Runoff." <u>National Geographic</u>, Feb. 1996: 106-125.

6. **An article in a weekly magazine**

Lave, Tamara Rice. "Equal Before the Law." <u>Newsweek</u>, 13 Jul. 1998: 14.

7. An article from a daily newspaper

Mayer, Nancy. "Dollars for Scholars?" The Oregonian, 25 Jan. 1996: C1, C5.

8. An editorial

"Lesson Plan for the City." Editorial. The Oregonian, 26 Jan. 1996: C12.

9. A letter to the editor

Luna, Ricardo V. Letter. The New York Times, 24 Jan. 1996: A14.

10. An article by an unknown author

"Americans Are Worried about the Safety of Their Drinking Water." National Wildlife, Feb./Mar. 1990: 48.

11. An article from NewsBank

Vobejda, Barbara. "U.S. Reports Decline in Poverty Rate." Washington Post, 6 Oct., 1995. Newsbank: Welfare and Social Problems 27 (1995): fiche 2, grids B7-B8.

12. An article from EbscoHost

Budge, David. "Organized Confucians." Times Educational Supplement 27 Oct. 1995: 10. 17 Nov. 1997. EbscoHost. Online. Ebsco Publishing.

(The second date is the day that you accessed the information)

13. An article in an online magazine or newspaper

"Kids Today Tuckered Out by T.V., Not Sports." The Japan Times Online 3 Dec. 1998. 13 Jan. 1999 <http://www.japantimes.co.jp/news/news12-98/news.html#story6>.

(The second date is the day that you accessed the information)

14. An online personal or professional web page

<u>Inherited Disease Genes Identified by Positional Cloning</u>. National Human Genome Research Institute. 26 Jan. 1999 <http://genome.nhgri.nih.gov/clone/>.

(The date is the day that you accessed the information)

15. An entry in an encyclopedia

"Mental Illness." <u>Encyclopedia Americana</u>. 1989 ed.

16. A reference on CD-ROM

"Equal Rights Amendment." <u>The 1996 Grolier Multimedia Encyclopedia</u>. Vers. 8.0. CD-ROM. Grolier Electronic Publishing, 1996.

17. A T.V. documentary program

<u>The Living Clock</u>. Narr. Richard Crenna. Writ. and prod. Gail Willumsen. The Infinite Voyage. PBS. WQED, Pittsburgh. 24 Sep. 1989.

18. A T.V. news story

Straight, George, rep. Teenagers with AIDS. <u>World News Tonight</u> with Peter Jennings. ABC News. 4 Jun. 1991.

19. A sacred writing

The Holy Bible. King James version. Book of Genesis.

20. A personal interview

Clarke, Robert E. Personal interview. 15 Aug. 1998.

Please note the **punctuation** for all types of entries. See the example of a research paper, beginning on page 103, for a complete student research paper with a list of works cited.

Below is a sample entry for a periodical:

        1   2   3   4

Cole, Wendy. "Perils of the Simple Life." <u>Time</u>, 6 Nov. 1995: 64-65.
           5

    1. Name of author (last name first)
    2. Title of the article (in quotation marks)
    3. Name of the periodical (underlined)
    4. Date of the periodical
    5. Page numbers of the article

Here is a citation for an article from EbscoHost:

      1   2   3   4

Cowley, Geoffrey. "The Future of Birth." <u>Newsweek</u>, 6 Nov. 1995. 14 Sep. 1998. EbscoHost. Online. Ebsco Publishing.
                               5   6

    1. Name of author (last name first)
    2. Title of the article (in quotation marks)
    3. Name of the periodical (underlined)
    4. Date of the periodical
    5. The date that you accessed this information
    6. Information about the online periodical index

And below is a citation from an article in an online newspaper:

      1   2

Kolata, Gina. "Mouse Study Fails to Verify Evolutionary Theory." <u>The New York Times on the Web</u>   3
  4 & 5 **1 Dec. 1998. 4 Dec. 1998 <http://www.nytimes.com/library/national/science/12098sci-health-imprint.html>.**
                                                     6

    1. Name of author (last name first)
    2. Title of the article (in quotation marks)
    3. Name of the periodical (underlined)
    4. Date of the periodical
    5. The date that you accessed this information
    6. The URL (Universal Reference Locator) for this web page

Research Paper Proposal

Before beginning a research paper project, you should at least have some idea of what you want to write about. Reading and other research will help you to develop your initial ideas into a real paper.

Take some time before you begin your research to write down some ideas on this page:

Proposal for research paper

1. Topic

I want to write about the following topic (_____
_____)

because _____
_____ .

2. Stand

I have the following opinion(s) about this topic: _____
_____

because _____
_____

3. Tentative thesis statement

_____
_____
_____

Review of steps in preparing the research paper

I. Select a topic.

II. Narrow the topic.

III. Find suitable sources: using the library, conducting interviews, etc.

IV. Take notes from the sources.

V. Using the notes and your own ideas, write an outline.

VI. Prepare the thesis statement.

VII. Write the "rough" draft, with introduction, body paragraphs, and conclusion.

VIII. Correct the "rough" draft and type a second draft.

IX. Type the final draft, including the list of works cited.

On the following pages, you will find an example of a student research paper.

Vanessa Harding

ENL 262

Instructor: John Sparks

June 4th, 1997

T.V. Ratings in Our Home

TV ratings have been on American television since 1997. They warn parents about the content of the programs that their children are about to watch. Jack Valenti, President of the Motion Picture Association of America (M.P.A.A.), invented the system with the approval of President Clinton. In the future, the V-chip, which will permit parents to block a program that they disapprove of, will be installed. The concern is about the wrong message that television is sending to children, and the effect it will have upon them. However, the problem is not which programs the children will watch, but whether the parents let them watch them. Television programs shouldn't have ratings because parents should be given more credit for their ability to raise their children.

American television presents a lot of different channels so that everybody can find what they like when they turn on the TV. What would be the point of having so many choices if those choices must be controlled? The ratings system outrages me as an adult because it makes me feel like a child being spied upon. It invades the privacy of my home without being wanted. The M.P.A.A. decided that the producers and distributors of shows will be the same people doing the ratings. Will those people be able to be impartial in their duty, and what kind of qualifications do they have to be the entities who are supposed to help us raise our children? Hollywood executives want to fight the ratings, and more specifically the V-chip, as an "intrusion into freedom of expression" because they are afraid some sponsors may want to be more selective about which programs they advertise on (Impoco 37).

Children may also be seduced by a strong rating. Dr. Cantor, Professor of Communication Arts at the University of Wisconsin, agrees that "both . . . age-based rating . . . and labels that said 'parental discretion advised' more often attracted children to a program than labels identifying a program as having 'mild violence' or 'graphic violence'" (Mifflin A17). The children probably don't know what 'mild' or 'graphic' violence is, but are taught that they are not supposed to watch PG-13 or R-rated programs. Furthermore, they may want to know what is behind those ratings and watch a show that they would never have thought about before. It is very easy to tempt a child; at school and with their friends, they hear a lot about violent shows or cartoons. They want to see them and to talk about them as well. With the help of a ratings system, they don't need anybody to help them find these shows. The ratings are written in the TV guide and shown on the top of the screen for the first fifteen minutes of a program.

One of the aspects that opponents of the system are concerned about is the judgment of the M.P.A.A. when it comes to sex and violence. What may be rude and unacceptable for some parents may be fine for others. As Jim Impoco underlines in his article, "All violence is not equal and . . . there is a difference between gratuitous violence and the scenes of prisoners being shot in Schindler's List that teach a powerful moral lesson" (38). He also notices that the V-chip will not be able to know if the rating means a violent police show or something that is more educational, but which contains violence. Therefore, if the parents don't double-check, they may prevent their children from watching a lot of very interesting historical programs.

Finally, what detractors have against the ratings system is that it tempts parents to let go of their responsibilities when it comes to television. Ken Conrad, senior Democrat from North Dakota, says: " . . . the networks, not the parents, decide what's best for every age group" (Gruenwald 424). Each parent has a different approach to violence, sex, or bad language, and for the networks to censor those is not the best solution. Children will be in contact with those 'undesirable' scenes while at friends' houses or when they are alone. Parents should explain to children that what they see on movies, shows, or cartoons is not real, that it is pure fiction invented to entertain people. Tehy should teach them to understand what they are watching instead of hiding it from them. Children are mart and always find a way to do what parents forbid. An explanation would be more efficient when it comes to violence, sex, and bad language. The children will be exposed to those problems sometime in their lives and, by knowing them and understanding them through the television and their parents, they will be armed to deal with them.

On the other hand, there are many parents who support the M.L.A.A. They claim that the ratings system will help them control what their children are watching while they are alone. Those parents don't want to be worried about what their children may see or hear, and they use the TV and ratings, along with the V-chip, to help to educate their children. If the parents program the V-chip and " . . . a child tries to disconnect or bypass the controller, . . . power is cut off to the TV and a flashing light alerts the parents" (Cohen 6). Those parents should have more faith in their children. They should trust them and give them more responsibility with their own education. For example, my uncle doesn't want his seven-year-old daughter to watch Channel One on French television. I was watching TV with her once, and I turned on Channel One. She asked me to change it.

Even young children understand what is good for them, and parents should give them credit for it.

The M.P.A.A. says that parents have the choice about whether to use the ratings system or not. They say that they are merely prosing their recommendation, but that parents still have the last word: "It identifies the violence, but it does not remove it. It puts the onus on the parents" (Zuckerman 64). Then the parents have two choices: blocking every program with a 'bad' rating or sitting down with their children and spending time explaining why they can't watch a specific program.

Jack Valenti, representing the entertainment industry, stated at the end of a White House session: "There has to be some kind of renaissance of individual responsibility that's accepted by parents, by the church, and by the schools, so that you build inside a youngster what we call a moral shield - it's fortified by the Ten Commandments of God - so that that child understands what is right and what is clearly wrong" (Mitchell B14). Mr. Valenti here seems to be surpassing his rights by using his beliefs to create a system based on the Bible. Parents should be given more credit and, instead of using a system created by conservatives, should go forward and explain the violence that their children might encounter.

Works Cited

Cohen, Sarah. "Trial TV Rating System Starts Amid Controversy." <u>Electronic News</u>. Jan. 6, 1997: 6.

Gruenwald, Julianna. "Critics Say TV Ratings System Doesn't Tell the Whole Story." <u>Congressional Quarterly Weekly Report</u>. Feb. 15, 1997: 424.

Impoco, Jim. "Another View of TV Ratings." <u>US News and World Report</u>. Feb. 19, 1997: 37.

Mifflin, Lawry. "TV Ratings System May Actually Lure to Violent Shows." <u>New York Times</u>. Mar. 27, 1997: A17.

Mitchell, Alison. "TV Executives Promise Clinton a Violence Ratings System by '97." <u>New York Times</u>. Mar. 1, 1996: B14.

Zuckerman, Mortimer B. "The Victims of TV Violence." <u>US News and World Report</u>. Aug. 2, 1993: 64.